TO AMERICA WITH LOVE

TO AMERICA WITH LOVE:
Letters From The Underground
by Anita and Abbie Hoffman

STONEHILL PUBLISHING COMPANY, NEW YORK

ISBN: 0-88373-044-8 (hardcover)
ISBN: 0-88373-052-9 (softcover)
Library of Congress Catalog Card Number: 76-6709

Book Design by Esther Mitgang
Cover illustration by Ron Lieberman

Photos: Abbie Hoffman by Angel; Anita and america
Hoffman by Lorey Sebastian.

First Printing.

Printed in the USA.

To two people whose help, dedication and love made this book, and a lot of other things, possible. They know who they are.

Nothing is more precious than independence and freedom.

—Ho Chi Minh

On August 28, 1973, Abbie was arrested and charged with selling cocaine to a police undercover agent. He faced a mandatory sentence of twenty-five years to life imprisonment, and the following April he disappeared and became a fugitive from the United States government. Abbie has long been a target of government police agencies because of his well-known civil-rights and antiwar activism. We now have evidence showing he was under illegal surveillance for months preceding the bust, and we believe he was set up for political reasons, but so far we have been unable to prove this conclusively in court.

Abbie, I am happy to say, is still at large. I live with our four-year-old son, america, in New York City. Obviously our lives have been deeply affected by these events. You could say our family was smashed by the State. On the other hand, families left and right are being smashed these days by forces stronger than the State, forces arising out of changed consciousness and changing mores. I would like to believe we are not so different from other downwardly mobile, disappearing families on the American scene. Our forced separation has enabled each of us to grow in ways not possible if we had been together.

The letters in this book span the first year of our separation and the eighth year of our marriage. They were our only link after Abbie split, the only reality we could share. Abbie's were written in unknown places in moments of privacy and solitude, mine were usually written in the last minutes of a hectic day. We fight, we manipuate, we brag, we complain and we make love in these letters. They weren't written with a view toward publication; that idea came to us last spring when security precautions ruled out further correspondence. When I reread the letters at Abbie's suggestion I experienced many emotions but the overriding sensation was of time travel. I saw patterns in our lives, stages of parallel growth, which neither of us had been aware of at the time.

The letters have been edited and arranged in loose chronological sequence. This creates occasional lapses in the continuity of our dialogue because letters were not always received in chronological order. We usually received letters within three to six days of the date they were written, but sometimes there were long delays and then we received three or four letters at once. These time lags prevented us from noticing certain coincidences of moods, ideas and events, which become apparent when the letters are read in chronological order.

Almost everyone referred to in the original letters, except for the three of us, was given a permanent code name for security reasons. I've now been able to convert many of them back to the real names. I have also added footnotes where necessary to clarify references in the letters.

Abbie and I avoided fixed names for ourselves, preferring to sign off according to our moods. In my more manic states I remember using Cleopatra, Joan of Arc, Sappho and Emma; in depressed moods I used the first female name that came to mind, like Minnie Mouse. Abbie did not restrict himself by gender or metaphysical category; his signatures included Fanny Hill, David Cassidy, Bluebeard, celery and Remy Martin, VSOP. As for our son, america, we never made a conscious decision about it, but neither of us could bring ourselves to call him by another name. He was only two and a half when we started corresponding and I think we were reluctant to alter his fledgling identity even figuratively. He is usually referred to as "the kid" or "junior." How could we call him Tommy or

Herbert when he was named after The Big Dream? He loves his name. We're gonna teach him the bad guys can never win as long as you hold onto your dreams . . . but I don't want to give away the plot!

            —Anita Hoffman

March, 1976

LETTERS FROM THE UNDERGROUND

Hello Anita!

It's me your friend all alone sitting in the middle of the loneliest universe one could imagine, but getting by. It's very hard to write to you. How open? How many facts? Security. My emotional state. I long to hear from you and yet I'm not sure. How should I spend my nights except in thoughts of you, of us, of the three of us. This is certainly my trial by fire, as well as yours. I'm completely alone now. I had to vacate the first place for many reasons, mostly I was not becoming someone else and spent too much time going over the past which hangs like a yoke around my neck. I've tried to write, to puzzle out some future, to plan security. Every step is difficult. Haunting nightmares of doors being kicked in, of police, and more, of jealousies. Missing you terribly, missing the kid each time I see one his age bouncing in the park on his father's shoulders. I was surrounded by that scene yesterday and almost in tears. I spent the entire day in bed trying to sleep it off so to speak. Today started afresh though. New hopes, a new location, a new name, some good steps. I've made numerous mistakes. However I must have done one thing right because from all appearances it seems my number hasn't come up yet. One haunting fear was that what if it was all a bad dream and there I was totally adrift, alone, fearing any contact with anyone that knew me and meanwhile everyone was trying desperately to contact me but not knowing how. Of course that's stupid but this life I'm stuck living produces weird thoughts. Chaotic thoughts. Imagine living in constant fear of being recognized and yet finding it extremely difficult to be alone, wanting to make friends but realizing you can only allow yourself the most superficial relationships possible.

God does appearance count! Only as an actor, I suppose, can one indulge in such displays of vanity. I must spend an hour a day on my appearance. I'm so fucking neat! It's a good thing I have time. I have to learn to take things slow. To have no expectations about life, about sanctuary, about a cause. Sheeet. I want to write so badly. Yet somehow the pattern, the style, the mood has not jelled. Should I do autobiography and stop at disappearance? Do I dare to write about now? Safely? What attitude? Wise guy? Lonely lovesick adolescent? Tired radical? Lazy one growing old anxiously awaiting death— hopefully in some quick, violent form. And what of my reaction when I hear of you? How should I react to bits of news? Could I actually die of a broken heart? Am I that romantically inclined? Can I not rationalize you away? What matters?

Am I a lesser man that George Wallace, than prisoners, than some crazy Jap who goes thirty years in the jungle for honor. Or than this weirdo chap in England, called the Elephant Man, turn of the century, who was reported to be the ugliest human ever to live. So ugly he had to make a special black cape and hood with tiny slits in to see out of, that completely covered his body so no one could see him. I read about him in one of my favorite books called *The Special People* by someone I think named Drimmer. It's all about history's famous freaks. Tom Thumb, giants, fat ladies, the Mule Faced Woman, Siamese twins, people with tails. You'd love the book and I really recommend it. It's a fantastic up! Great photos!

I have some good tapes with me, listen a lot—like Yellow Brick Road album by Elton John. Read Mailer's Monroe book and when I finished it she seemed diminished in my eyes concerning her talent. I think it got inflated after the fact of her death, I mean. About Mailer, well, he can write all right. I envy any writer that can hold a thought longer than a minute. That has the tenacity to pick a subject and think it through, twisting and turning its jaded mysteries in one's mind and penning them coherently. God I wish I could write. I think I am a lazy sonofabitch. Egomaniacal to the point where I feel each step I take, each sight I see, each thought is fresh, unique, and to stop, sit back, observe, would be to cease to perform and somewhere I've equated performing with life itself. Which of course makes this little assignment, namely, being other people for the next thirty years or so, such a mind fuck.

I feel a compelling urge to write you yet I'm afraid how I'll react to letters from you. Will they make me homesick? Jealous? Proud? What news of the kid? It's all so confusing. There you are trying to be noticed as an individual, accepted on your own for who you are. And here I am trying to lose myself, to not be recognized. To become a nobody, or well, average.

I think we are one of the greatest love stories of this or any other time. No matter what happens. Yet what exactly is Love in this time of ours? Everything changes so rapidly. As to the future, from my side of the aisle you are equated with happiness, or to make it clearer, life over the past seven years has on balance been equated with the ultimate joy of my life. There is no way we could safely be together even if your feelings toward me were different. We are doing what has to be done in order to survive and perhaps gain another few rounds of happiness before chug-a-lugging the old hemlock. You must not be afraid of hurting my feelings. A long time will have passed. Things will change. Try to be honest.

Today has been a good day. It is very beautiful where I am. I am learning much about life and myself. Really growing when everything goes O.K. but I realize my life is so fragile. There was that moment back in the other place where I ventured out onto this beautiful hilltop when this drug-whacked-

out hippie kid—the stereotype of a million "far-fuckin-outers"
—did a double take and said, "Hey, I know who you are."
Then he approached and I extended my hand and spoke in this
strange tongue (it was like in *The Exorcist*) which I couldn't
even imitate now but we had a little chat and it was over. And
I felt 90 percent that I had pulled it off O.K. But I was numb
the whole time. Little scene like that had to be the best performance of my life. It had better have been good. I left the next
day. Goddamn hippies got all the best seats on the planet.
That's the kind of shit that really gets to you knowing it
isn't just the coppers you have to contend with. It's the inno-
cents who are just looking for a good story to tell, not knowing
the effect it has on someone in my condition. I mean time froze.
I moved and changed my appearance.

I made a friend, though, a nice guy who knows a lot of
actors. We got on well together and I asked him what it takes
to be a great actor. I mean, what are the people like inside.
He said, "Inside they are nothing." Babes, I don't think I can
act a damn. I think I am the exact opposite of a yoga state.
I mean my mind just never relaxes. It just shifts from one area
to another but it never stops. My best disguise would be a
frontal lobotomy.

By the by, knew a psychoanalyst once who wanted to drop
out and establish an exotic retreat for folks who wanted to kill
themselves in some grand style à la George Sanders renting a
castle in Spain or the film *Grand Bouffe*. He wants to call the
place "The Last Resort." Well, I'm rattling on too much for
openers.

Hope the bad weather isn't getting you down. Hope america's
health is doing well. I feel ashamed of hurting him the slightest.
He is just such a great person and I miss his ecstasy over
discovering a new phase, developing a new facet of personality.
God, that scene on the beach. We were both so wrecked on the
dope and tired and you going one way and me the other and

pulling the kid apart. Nothing like that had ever happened to us. To all of us I mean. It's the stuff Freud wrote about, I'm sure. God, it scared me. Imagine what it did to the kid, and I see how it happened. I understand it. I understand why those POWs in North Vietnam had to be programmed on reentry about family matters. There was a simple matter of responsibility over the decision making. You had just gone through the ordeal of the apartment in New York (great job—you've always been a champion nest builder)—for you and the kid. That was now your basic unit and there I was playing father as if we were back in the calm of Louse Point on Long Island where I probably, oh I am sure, yes, went swimming more with the kid than you did. Oh I am sure of it. So there was a breakdown in communication and sparks flew just for a few seconds. It's a trauma none of us will forget easily. I feel sorry for those POWs. I feel sorry for all people that go to war, go to prison, get bad diseases, have physical handicaps, have their dreams destroyed. I think I'm just beginning to learn about much of the human experience. I think I can honestly say I never really understood what sadness meant. Tragedy is so distant from my experience in life. I am digging in for the long haul.

You are forever with me. I wish there was something, some way of explaining this to the kid. If there's anything you can think of in this regard I would be most cooperative. This part hurts, hon. I have to stop. Thanks for being nice to me our last day together. It helped a lot.

> Take care and love to 'merica,
> your pen pal

Darling:

I finally got your first letter. I am sad. It sounds harder than I imagined for you. I guess the only way the past few months have been bearable for me was the belief in your confidence. The belief I did not have to worry on your score, except for your health. Now that belief is shattered and I feel almost as lonely as you sound. I'm not so lonely 'cause I am among our friends but I want to comfort you, if I can.

Do you know I said in my press statement the same thing you wrote in your letter, that the past seven years have been the happiest of my life. I think I put it in there wanting you to hear it, to be reminded of my love. Yes, I had a press conference last week after arrest warrants were issued for you when you failed to show for a hearing. I read a four-page, closely typed statement, which I worked hard on. I'm sending it separately. There weren't too many questions afterward because, Mayer says, it was obvious I wasn't going to divulge your whereabouts—which I'm relieved I don't know. The general reaction of friends and acquaintances seems to be "good for him, I'm glad he's out of danger," although not many people say anything directly to me about you. It's their way of being cool, I know.

There is interesting news about your dope bust setup. It was apparently planned far more elaborately than I, at least, had suspected. We have recently gotten word that you were being watched months before the bust and wiretapped at my mother's old apartment, when you stayed there. The lawyers are going to hire an investigator to check this out. I will keep you informed.

I have not been visited or noticeably harassed but I'm keeping a sharp eye. The first call I got when I came home from the press conference was Master Charge! I guess you've been put on the Big Computer, honey. You should see my mail—it's all bills. I've started a file for unpaid bills. Someone told me that's what you're supposed to do! It's already bulging of course.

My money situation is bad so I have to make decisions about where to put my energy. Whether to work on a book for teenagers or hurry into a stifling job. And which job? No matter how I figure it, I can't seem to cover the costs of food, rent and daycare. If the job hours overlap his daycare I would be working at a deficit since I would have to shell out mon again for babysitters. I'm considering doing a short, concise autobiography of the past seven years and calling it "(you), me and america." I don't want to. My heart's desire is not to write about us, but other kinds of books take too long to sell and a job may not be practical for me, with junior and all. I'll figure it out. I know for certain I'll be a whore before I'll be a secretary again. I couldn't even afford to be a secretary, anyway, with daycare expenses.

I have problems and down moments, just like you. It's a struggle, the core often seems to be struggle. Now that I must live like a man I can scarcely admit to feeling down or scared or indecisive. There is no one I can confide in. Generally speaking, I'm managing. I feel loved by the outside world and stay busy workwise and socially. But yesterday morning I considered shooting myself. I was to start writing the book proposal and the kid became ill with bronchitis, in total misery, keeping me up day and night. He's had a bad cough all winter and been sick five or six times, each time when I have had important things to do. Each time my resistance to it lowers. I want to run out of the house, keep running and running and not hear him cry and make demands of me. Just keep running away. And I know I never can. Even when he is well I am free of him for such short periods. I love him and I know it's not his fault, it's just hard.

He's better today. I feel so sorry for him sometimes. I am his whole world. It makes me feel sad and guilty. I worry about not having the physical strength for all that is required of me. He talks about you and I encourage it. We have matter-of-fact conversations as though you were around the corner.

Maybe this can work out right and it's the best situation. If I can conquer my present problems there'll be no stopping me. I'll have won a happiness I didn't deserve before, if that makes sense.

The other night I met Ron Kovic, a young organizer in the veterans' movement who was severely disabled in the Vietnam war. Know what he said to me? "A - - - - must be great. He must be just like you." Nobody's ever said that to me. What a super compliment.

You are not alone babes. I share a secret part of my life with you. I hope that's O.K. because I probably make conditions sound worse than they are. Don't worry. We're O.K. and getting better. I should rewrite this but I'm tired and want to mail it soon. That wuz yesterday I wuz talking about. Tomorrow looms ahead full of promises of new complications and further impediments about to fall on my head.

Believe it or not, I'm trying to have a good time!

—your co-conspirator in subversive love.

Dear,

The FBI visited me last week. They said I should call them when you call me! They wanted to know if you were sending me money and if you had a Swiss girlfriend!! I said, "A Swiss girlfriend! I wish he had a Swiss bank account!" They asked some weirdo questions which made me wonder where they get their information.

A few days later we went to the country to get some belongings and the feds were there too. I drove out to make a phone call, leaving the kid with a friend in the house, when a car pulled out of the dirt road in the woods, following me. I wasn't sure it was really following me, but suddenly the entire grillwork of the car started flashing red, so I pulled over to the side of the road. I was stoned on mescaline and all I could think was, gee, I've still never taken a trip without any paranoid incidents. It turned out he was the county sheriff and he was looking for you. He said the FBI was in town and he wanted to bring me in for questioning. He wouldn't even let me go back to the house first to tell my friend and the kid. I told him that was ridiculous because they expected me back in five minutes. Then the police chief arrived and he asked me if you were in the area. I gazed at the gray and silent woods which seemed to shimmer, and I said, "I really don't know. I doubt it. But he sure liked it here." The police chief said I could go back to the house and they would visit me there, if necessary. When I got home we saw a car parked out in the woods. It stayed there all night, and in the morning, when we left, two cop cars intercepted us on the road out of town.

Strange, it had just been an O.K. mescaline trip before the cops intervened, but they brought it up to the level of our old trips together. Got the adrenalin flowing. I still like the drama, damn it. I'm psychologically addicted to you, you adventurer!

Then, that same day, Sunday, they knew I wasn't home in New York, so seven FBI agents came to the apartment, threatening to break the door down. No warrant, of course. Jackie was in the apartment. She got scared and let them in. They opened the closets and refrigerator, searching for a body. I was pissed she let them in, but she freaked.

The kid is suddenly big and feisty and talkative. He looks like you. I wish you were here for his peepee instructions. You would adore him now—he's old enough to be obnoxious when he wants. I do love him. I'm glad I have him, then I am never totally alone.

I could believe in your love for me more if it was because I was such a great individual rather than a familiar glove. Don't try to hurt me in your letters and I won't try either. How can you be jealous of me when all the position I occupy in the world is because of you? I just want to do better than that so I can be proud of myself. Maybe then you will be too.

Got your letter of May 7 today and should wait to write
(other things to do) but got so excited I just had to be in
contact. It was a wonderful letter. I save them all, as I've
told you.

First off, I doubt they can find me. Loneliness is a problem
but the challenge and the confrontation with yourself are exhilarating. Many of your letters have referred to this business
of liking you as a "glove" rather than as an individual. Well,
every set of gloves I ever owned I lost within a week. A glove
is a mini-prison, you can't make love with gloves, you can't
write. Sheeet, you can't even pick your nose! So what the hell
good is a glove. I have compared you loads of times to many
women I've known (and men, too) before and after the bust.
And some are incredibly fascinating with umpteen million
skills, attributes, in all shapes and sizes. Besides I am also
aware of some of your activities and am not jealous. Mostly
I see us as part of a huge incestuous family, so everything is
O.K. both ways in that regard. The fact of the matter is, I
love you. Romantically if you will. And although I can relate
to large-family concept I still am traditionally romantically in
love with you. And I love you because you don't bore me over
the long run.

Take our life on St. Thomas two years ago. I could never—
not with the most luscious of swivel-hipped sweeties, spend six
months on an island without desperately fighting for my own
space. Also I was at a strange point then. I had another choice
and actually wasn't all that hot for you. It was the period
when you seemed most like a glove. But I'm glad I went and
I'm glad of everything. I don't even care about the bust. I

never have flashbacks to the event ("Oh, if this didn't happen,
what a life."), I swear, I never get into that.

This is a totally absorbing adventure and I'm handling it
O.K., given certain personality facets which contrast with this
lifestyle: bragging, performing, witty, all that stuff. But after
all I love performing for you and of course our little friend,
the most, and could really go the long distance that way quite
happily. This time apart will be great for you to see from
others' feedback that you really have something on the ball.
Never let people convince you that "reality" must be faced.
Make up your own reality and do not abandon Romance. If I
am to gó down, why not on the Ship of Love? And look at our
third partner. By the way, I could not just shut him out of
my mind. In fact you really can't shut people out of your
mind. It's the old psych. experiment of trying to unlearn "the"
by typing "teh" a thousand times a day. Each time you hit the
old keys "the" gets reinforced. At first I thought, hey, I could
go the whole route, no contact with anyone ever again. Yes,
that seemed the most courageous and safest and smartest.
After all, even this letter has an aftereffect on me for days.
Wondering about its route, each thing I've scrawled. But I am
down on some days and need "fixes" from the past.

So much hubbub with coppers. I figure they will exert a lot
of energy tracking down bizarre leads for another month or so
and then decide I'm not worth it. Remember, I don't even know
your address, as you don't know mine. Imagine you yourself
have seen half a dozen or more feds. But they have a lot more
important things and will forget it soon. The FBI is hoping for
two things. I'll pull some robbery needing money and get
caught, or someone will get in trouble and snitch me out.
They could never rely on their own manpower. They are
tricky though. The girlfriend part was added to get a reaction
from you. Do you understand what I mean? They might also lay
a heavy rap on you hoping to follow you the next day,

figuring you'll call me. Remember these guys are real straight arrow in their thinking.

But my position is real. This is not a pose. A car pulls up at night, a glance in the street, a few misspoken words, that's all real, and fear is real, not imagined. I'm incredibly vulnerable, like a flower growing on a highway. One jerk of some truckdriver's wheel and *au revoir*. I think perhaps you are one of the few people I know who would also prefer death to prison. Luv, luv, luv. Thus the frailty of existence is real, and people will want to help a lot, but that's accepted. They must also come to understand that I was set up. I would have written a piece already regarding the circumstances if it wasn't for the others involved, the ones awaiting trial. Somehow people aren't getting that point.

Now I've taken steps in a number of directions: "settling down," a secret interview and a revolutionary career that would be very political. The third occupies a lot of my thinking and I have an incredible plan. It needs some more changes in me and contacts that will take a while, but it's solid and has a lot of appeal. I think about groups and people in similar situations and see all the problems clearer now. There seems to me a certain revolutionary suicide strain in my plan. It's not obviously as safe as another route. But I've always been willing to do this for the right cause and nothing has changed that. The difference between this year, say, and last year in my life, was last year I couldn't see that road at all, it seemed wiped out. Being alone and hunted has forced me to examine my political side much more than rolling around the hay with our friends did. The way someone dies is as important as how they live. I think that's a real macho attitude toward life but I believe it. My father died as he lived. This doesn't mean having to cast your blood on the barricades, so to speak. No, that's not what I'm getting at. But *morality* is, I think, your old-fashioned stand-by. For me, anyway. I can think of no better reason to give one's life to the earth than to try and make the world a better place to live in, and I don't mean planting flowers on Mother's Day or bandaging the wounds of beggars in the streets of Calcutta. I mean Revolution. Violent Revolution. That's in the cards.

Ah shit, babes, I want to tell you *all* my stories. One just happened. I was in a room where there was a discussion about me. I can't, of course, get into everything. I would just burst like a bubble and write things I'm not supposed to.

I've made mistakes and am absent-minded, but I have corrected some things. For example, I think there are two kinds of people in the streets. There are the people who "hunt" with their eyes and people who "hide." I noticed that I had a habit of staring people in the eyes. I think it's an outgrowth of either performance syndrome, always on the make, or not being afraid of the world. In a word, not being uptight about staring the world in the eyes. It might also be a fame leftover. In any event it's extrovert rather than introvert. I've corrected it, and now avoiding eye contact like that is instinctive.

There are so many little things. The operation helped. I probably look the same (there's no one to ask) but it's given me a serious attitude. Also I now work all day. I've had this job for almost a month now and have made it a point to show up on time and put some energy into it. I've enrolled in classes at night but can't say much except that it has political content. I'll tell you more about the job later. But you should know I'm keeping real busy, busy.

So many activities to tell you about. Last night was the benefit for Chile which Phil Ochs has been working on. He did a magnificent job. It was a sell-out and fantastically moving. Even Bob Dylan came. Many old comrades whom I hadn't seen in years were there. I kept wishing you could have been there, for it would have recharged your batteries and given you inspiration to go on. Paul Krassner was sure he saw you in the audience!

There was a film about Victor Jara, the folksinger whom Stew and Jerry met when they went to Chile during the Allende days. Victor was murdered in the National Satdium in Santiago. The accounts say the military chopped off his fingers and beat him in front of six thousand prisoners in the stadium, but Victor rose up and began to sing the anthem of the Unidad Popular. The prisoners joined in, and Victor was shot. His English widow was at the benefit with their two small children. She gave a short speech and then translated his song as he performed on the screen, strumming his guitar. The music was soft and sweet, a ballad he had written in Spanish. He would sing a line, then she would translate. It seemed to me they were making love together a final time. I felt honored to meet her afterward.

After the benefit there was a party with a lot of celebrities and assorted glamorous or powerful people. The type of party I used to hate, but I had a good time. I was introduced to Bob Dylan and started to tell him of your regrets about demonstrating in front of his house that time, but after two minutes someone grabbed him, and a crowd gathered, and I never saw him again. The way the crowd descended upon him made me think he was justified in any paranoia he feels. He was small and fragile, like a yeshiva boy.

The afternoon before the benefit I went to see Noah [Kimerling], the accountant. He says there's a big fight with the IRS coming up over the donation you gave the Black Panthers in 1970. They are charging us with owing them $7,600 on the $22,000 you gave to the Panther bail fund (which was forfeited). Of course we are contesting it, but I worry about the IRS prowling around or seizing our TV—the only thing we have of value.

I also appeared on a small cable TV show the night before the benefit. I was very nervous although Mayer, who had arranged it, tried to reassure me beforehand. It's hard appearing for someone else—the old Abigail McCarthy trip. I was uncomfortable being interviewed as "wife of." I hope I did O.K. I'll see it next week.

Received your May 10 letter and loved it. Sorry to miss that benefit. I feel close to it. Just read the article on the death of Victor Jara. God, such beasts exist. So sad, so heroic. I feel like a shit heel next to such bravery. I'm enclosing a poem I wrote—use it however you want. You know that blue coat I have, the one my friend Jimmy McCaan in Ireland gave me? Well, he was killed too. Shot in the streets of Dublin. By the time it happened he had become an incredible folk-hero leader of the Provos. Sometime I'll tell you how I found out. Strange.

You don't seem to be aging or growing bitter. I think you have more character than me, actually. I keep picturing our roles reversed. God, I'd love to stage manage this whole thing. Wanted to do that for others and you, you'd make such a clever fugitive. You'd never get caught. Me, I'm not so sure. I'm careless, I don't get off on patience. I still gobble my food, lust for sex continually, write hundreds of words, do the book, work, study, read, exercise. I just don't know how to sit still. Always wanting the best of all worlds. What a little kid I am. Orphan of America.

Don't sweat the bread and don't be ashamed to borrow. I'm concerned about my next book. Here I am writing away and I'm not sure how it can ever be published. I don't understand IRS problem. You and I are separate under the law, no?

I'd love to see your writing. I have a problem since I like to polish my stuff after it's been typed and can't type (don't want to learn, either).

It's always best when writing to hold letter a day, then re-read. It's one of my better habits. Although I've already pulled some bits that no central committee would have ever tolerated.

17

Fuck'em. You think you get off on adventure. God, I think it's the only reason to be alive. I miss you though. I want to hug and squeeze you. I want to hear all the stories you tell so well. I want you to wave your left hand in the air, puffin on the butt, saying "no sweat" (it's your best line). I want to see it all. The longer we wait, of course, the better the show will be. Right? You are so beautiful tonight. I spent the whole night awake thinking of you.

love,
your erring knight.

For Joan Jara

Victor Jara's fingers lay throbbing in the midday
terror of a Chilean sun.
Groping for the string of freedom—
better it were a fuse igniting a thousand well-placed
bombs than a note of beauty vibrating through the misty
eyes of shattered dreams.
If I had one of his fingers, I'd curl it round the trigger
of a .45 and blast a hole in tyranny's wall.
I pray that I could have a hero's hand strong enough to
caress the memory of his death.
Can you find inside yourself the beast that cut
the poet's hand?
From what swamp spring such animals?
Uniformed mutations of life's pulsating ecstasy.
Please tell her his fingers have triggered me to keep
on going.
Tell her I'm sorry I slept late that day—and sorry
not to have helped.

Glad to hear everything going so smoothly. The meeting sounds tempting. I am definitely into a meeting in fall or winter and then a decision about us. If I get book contract I've promised myself a vacation in August or September.

I'm still waiting to hear from agent on book proposal. I did an interview with Joan Jara, which Leslie videotaped. But the magazine didn't want it, and I'm trying to place it elsewhere. Leslie and I are thinking of doing a series of video interviews with interesting women. Only I'm not sure how to sell them since her equipment is only black and white. There are so many things I want to do, but no money, and if the book contract doesn't come through I will have to consider a job again. I dread it because it would cut out anything interesting for me. There would be no time to write or interview or do things I can genuinely learn from. I was not so happy with this interview and realize I have much to learn, but doing it, and the book proposal, made me feel like a person.

I saw the cable TV show I was on. I thought I was boring and not very original. I'm not good speaking for you. I feel crippled by it.

Sometimes I think I can only join you if I fail. But then I think, how could I live with you who never fails. One thing I must keep remembering is your show-off quality. I more than anyone else know all you have to show off, but if life with you were to be always admiring your trip with none of my own, I don't think I could hack it. I don't want to be your appendage, part of your entourage in a life where friendships and an identity for myself are impossible. However, I think we're in a healthy stage: both can live without the other, and now are free to decide how much we want the other.

I'm glad you think of our child a lot. He mentions you all the time and I tell him how much you love him. He is so beautiful. He wears real jeans now and T-shirts and a baseball hat when not wearing the cowboy hat you gave him. I'm told that at school he is very gentle and the teachers were happy one day when he grabbed a doll back and bit his friend Emmy who is a terror. It was the first time he exhibited aggression. Everybody loves him. He's very affectionate and not a big complainer, even though he's sick again with a sore throat. Thanks for the gift for him. I had to spend it on doctor bills and medicine.

I am pretty alone when it gets down to the future. So much responsibility. If I were without the child I would not worry so much. No one knows this side of me except you. Everyone thinks I am managing so well. Your love is important to me, otherwise I would feel completely alone, in spite of junior. He is so cute lately I cannot express it except by grabbing him. If only I could train the little fucker to sleep late. Sometimes, in the morning, that seems the biggest problem I have!

It's raining. I've been writing all day. I have eighty-five pages in hand. The autobiography's going to be six hundred pages, I can sense it, and one big rewriting job. I'm just piling it all down. I'm very happy when I've worked on the auto, but have to pace myself because of my aching finger. I hold the pen in the strangest way and my penmanship stinks.

It was sad about the SLA today. Death by fire—what a quick life.

I love you very much bright eyes. Let's face it, this is pure love. I could never love you this much if you were lying here next to me. I keep giggling what could be a more perfect marriage. You have to admit we're not exactly crowding each other's space. I've heard of modern marriages with separate rooms, but this! This takes the Wedding Cake. I must finish this book before I see you. I must accomplish many things. I want to make you proud of me. Your keychain is the only thing I haven't lost. Oh, no, I still got the pajamas, and let's see, the bathrobe, my tape recorder which I am sexually in love with and a bunch of old writing which I sort through from time to time.

I want to tell you everything, goddamn it. Those fucking spies, why can't I just tell you everything. If only we were together in person. I guess I can tell you of brick busting. Imagine what a jerk-off, hon! Next time you pass a building check out what a brick looks and feels like. Now feel your hand on the side, so tender with all these little bones in there rattling around like it was windy Halloween. Next, picture placing the brick between two chairs. Measuring the distance carefully with your hand, and then ARRRRRGHHHUH! WOMP! I can really do it. I was studying karate for a while but had to stop. But I keep toughening my hands and mental attitude. Today I zonked a brick and felt I might try two next week. It's a whole Zen experience. Because you really have to get mentally set. If you pull up at the last minute and don't follow through you can break your hand. I'm sure. Oh god, I'd love to show the kid that trick. Don't be surprised when we meet if you see my hands all bandaged. Nothing more on the macho front to report. Still no word from agent 32 D. Portuguese wine tastes better than ever.

I've read the whole Nixon tapes. They are better than the Loud family. You should try to petition the FBI to get all the material wiretapped from us over the years. Saying they have violated copyright privileges by recording our lives without written consent. Say we'll settle out of court for a copy of the tapes. Dirty bastards. It's weird. I mean it's hard enough having to change your whole life but to know some day a few cars will pull up and an army of suits will jump out creating this beehive of activity on some peaceful little thoroughfare. Run, run, run, fast as you can. You can't catch me I'm de Gingerbread Man . . . . . . ech! They did catch him though and ate him up. How awful. I've always considered Gingerbread Men holy and could never eat one. I just let'em sit on the shelf till they get so hard they break if you lift'em up.

Babes, I feel bad not being able to help when the little one gets sick. It makes me really sad. Every time I think of him I get sad. Why is that? I wish I could find another way of feeling. Somehow I can't. I mean I feel real close to you. Through the letters and just all the memories, and anyway, you're an adult and all. But him . . . I'd like to show him the brick trick and see him in the cowboy hat. My only joy in that degree is that I don't have to look at him through bars on grimy windows. Remember those awful visits at the Tombs? Did you read where some BLA people tried to carve a hole in one of those booths with an acetylene torch but failed. They were trying to get Al Washington out. We were friends in the Tombs. It was a good idea. Alas! He's really beautiful. We played chess a lot. They captured him in San Francisco and brought him across country with a cocked gun held against his head in case anyone tried to rescue him. I think he went to Boston University.

Lo love,

News that you moved was a real jolt! * I'm really upset. I
know how much work you put into that place. Hey, hon, you
sure you're on the right track? If something happens to the little
one I feel responsible. Goddamn it. I happen not only to be your
husband and in love with you but the kid is my kid in every
sense of the word. I mean it and I'm mad I'm not taking care
of you better. I don't care about women's lib or anything. I
don't care if you are happy, I only care if you are in pain. The
scene where I am is terrific. You would have time to yourself.
I long to show you around, to hold your hand, to make you
proud to be my wife. I long to see the kid grow into a macho
little devil. If something happened to him in this period it
would be the greatest tragedy of our lives.

You're wasting a lot of time moving around like some scene
out of *Les Misérables.* It was O.K. knowing you were settled,
making friends, even fucking—I don't care. I just don't want
to see you alone and kid sick. Goddamn it, don't hurt yourself. I miss you for another reason, I trust you. I trust your
judgment, opinions, love and abilities. What exactly does New
York have for you anyway? I'll tell you something I held back.
You used to dread the Coretta King role—you ain't seen
nothing because ol' Mr. King was dead, he wasn't wandering
around the jungle, wasn't even in jail. I'll tell you another
thing, everyone I meet falls in love with me. Can you dig that!

* Abbie got this information from other sources. I had already
moved by the time the correspondence began, and since it was a *fait
accompli* it hadn't occurred to me to mention it in my letters.

I'm not bragging, really. It's a problem because I can't give totally of myself. I say my love died and I'm afraid, but that's worse—maternal shit comes out. Janis is wailing on the radio, "don't take your love from me, baby. Give while you can, hey, hey, hey. Don't turn your back on love. Get it while you can . . ."

You start laying out trips in your letters, maybe travel in the winter, maybe a book contract in the fall. You want my trip, O.K. In three months I'm off to the revolution, dig. So long, tootsie. Have a good time sipping cognac at Max's or losing your temper with the kid, or puffing your head off or filling out forms in employment offices or gossiping about who's screwing who.

I think our marriage was made in heaven and if you don't have plans to reunite or check it out in the next few months, let me know.

Maybe I'm a little hysterical and your situation ain't that bad. There are only three things I can't handle in life: harm to any one of us. Fuck all our friends, fuck the world. I LOVE YOU. I LOVE AMERICA.

MACHO

The child is still sick. I've been in the house ten days with him and now I'm getting sick. There is no longer money for babysitters and somehow friends can never help when you really need them. I cannot even go out to mail letters or buy a newspaper. We are almost out of money so many problems are buzzing around in my head, but in the presence of the child, thinking about problems is merely aggravating. I can only solve problems when he is asleep or out of my presence.

Your letter, a fine letter, came at a bad time for me! All I could see as the purpose of my life was being rid of the child and you presented me with ten more projects.* That, and your ridiculously risky letter to VN made me feel overwhelmed. I shall never escape the kid's owning half of me and you owning the other half. The conflict tears me apart. If only he would stay well and you would stay cautious. I will do whatever I must for both of you. I'll just have to prove I exist too, by becoming Superwoman.

Now that you are so up I worry more than when you were unsure and cautious. So do your friends. Your latest escapade, the letter to VN, really upset me. I dreamed you and I were shooting it out in an SLA-type scenario and that you got it. Then I dreamed the cops hated you so much they carried

* This refers to Abbie's letter of May 19, in which he requests me to do a number of things for him. Throughout this book we've omitted similar material partially for security reasons and also because the details are not terribly interesting. The requests ranged from consulting with lawyers about ongoing lawsuits to efforts to publish *Book of the Month Club Selection,* his latest book, to Abbie Hoffman and Friends Defense Committee projects, and such errands as sending him his underwear and tennis shoes.

your corpse around from precinct to precinct. Please. The situation is real enough. Please be careful.

The publishers are not interested in my book proposal. The magazines may be different so I'm working up article proposals. They will not take anything "political," only personal subjects. I'd like to do a good piece on Joan Jara, ending it with your poem, which is beautiful. It's the only one I'm really hot to do, but I don't know who would take it.

Since I don't know how long it will take to nail down a mag assignment, I'm applying for welfare as soon as I can get out of the house.

Even if I occasionally resent the public wife role I know that I would be a thousand times more miserable if I were not helping. Maybe you force out the best in me! Whatever it is that ties us together is stronger than ever. I don't know what it is, but I can see it will last a lifetime.

Why not learn to type? What have you got against it?

I came across a sentence you said, "I'd rather have my freedom than my friends."

Viva magazine wants me to write our love story for a grand. *Redbook* might be interested in "what it was like to experience the media trip," so I'm going through your old files to get my head in shape for writing a proposal. Each mag, by the way, wants their own ideas implemented and are cold to mine. Anyway, I found an old scrapbook which had clippings from your Worcester and Mississippi years. I read some long serious speeches on banning the bomb and pictured you lecturing to a church group wearing a suit or at least a sports jacket. I had forgotten how much you have done. So much imagination in one body, every interview so eloquent, so brilliant. I don't like me so much in those years. I feel shame because I felt lost, unsure, no identity. You always had a strong one. I think I needed to live desperately, wretchedly, without you in order to become a separate person. Can you understand?

You are such a great poet. Your letters are incredible. But sometimes they are so heavy they are like a weight on my chest.

You must not make too many demands on me. My days are filled with errands and the child; the nights with writing. I am always tired. I look haggard and have a cough which keeps me awake at night. I cannot do everything. Please, I am not like you. I have no freedom and it is not easy for me to survive. Do not ask too much. I do not have the time or the money to do everything you ask.*

I may not do love story for *Viva*. You've given me no time to think about it. If it's botched I'll never live it down. I need time to think and write and support myself. You take up whole days which I cannot afford. After the next project you must give me a rest. Space out the tasks or I cannot do them.

---

* I had received Abbie's letter of May 27, which is omitted here, but which contained more requests and suggestions.

High you,

Received May 20 letter. Mail is definitely a problem and correspondence extremely awkward with delays. It was sad to read your down letter, but understandable. I wrote you one once but tore it up. I've had so many bad breaks and am absolutely the world's worst fug, but somehow I'm managing to get off something fierce on this whole trip.

I feel close to you, hon. Every day. I don't understand your whole failure/success concepts. You write of me as "the one that never fails." It has an Indian ring to it—too godlike. I fail constantly, I can't figure out what you mean. In fact, I often see you as the big success, well, success in one area for sure, Ideas. You are totally at ease in the maze world of ideas. You have a rapier-quick mind. Smart as a whip. There's no idea anyone might lay on you that you couldn't flash on and challenge or elaborate. Me too. Guess that makes us intellectuals. Intellectuals get ideas and try to change life to fit ideas (the committed ones). There is another type, people who are at home in the world—the Adventurers. I love the family idea. Blending everyone's assets, info, talent, money, love, caring. I hope we can all pull it off. Global love nest perpetual incest.

I need more time, for what who knows? I know nothing. I'm only three months old. I'm making a good deal of progress. Loads of shit breaks. Hair problems. Every time it changes color I gotta make up mindass stories to go with it, and what the fuck do you do about split ends???? Do you think Che Guevara had to worry about split ends?

I know what you mean about friends boring. You gotta find ways to turn yourself on. Hey, I'm no one to give advice but I can't afford to whine over errors. Gotta keep going. I've had down times and moments of real ecstasy. Don't think it would be different in that regard if I were there with you in NY. Seems mood swings are the tempo of the times. Did you go to [*More*] convention? I would have enjoyed seeing David Bowie talk on "the New Boredom" to the minds. I want to be in very good form when we meet. Voice, looks, sense of mastering the situation. I'm getting there but I have a ways to go.

I hope you get your contract. I even hope you get to fall in love with other people. I don't feel particularly jealous in any possessive way, just miss your company. Besides, we can't repeat our relationship with others. Who would want to, anyway. I never said you'd find life boring without me, did I? What an egomaniac you married. Sorry to give you all those jerky tasks.

I hope you get to leave the city for a few months and forget about me. The Leopard is also changing his spots. Do what you want. I didn't like your cable TV show, just as you didn't. Best thing was your statement after bust and *New Yorker* article. Glad you like poem. Your letters scare me a little.

I don't want to spell out all my thoughts. My feelings toward you are much more complicated than when we were together. There's too much if we have to prove ourselves to each other. It's very grating. Times goes so slowly. I'm anxious to have a year go by to see what happens. I really get off on wondering where this is all leading. As soon as money starts to run out things will get really interesting, I suppose. I am seriously exploring the idea of joining a revolutionary group. I blow hot and cold on the idea but am laying groundwork with study. You can imagine how complicated such a decision is. I almost see it as a form of suicide. Yet, I'm not sure. I wonder about what people should do with their lives. Flash on your SLA

dream. Of course all that affected me greatly. The dead ones.
I don't see people dying in revolutionary battle as dying senseless deaths. As to all their fuck-ups, I guess I believe some of
them but sense a lot of the stories are fabricated.

The FBI wants certain images maintained and lies to the
press. Take my case. They have, I assume, put a price on my
head. I don't mean a reward offered on Post Office wall poster.
I mean the amount of money they will pay for info. Also in
terms of man hours they'll exert. Right now it's pretty high.
Considering this is just a local dope bust. The DA said this was
no unusual case. Bullshit. The FBI is on a vendetta. IRS too.
All of a sudden it's not allowed to give money to bail funds—
after three years. Why in this case? Others gave to the Panthers and lost money. They were never bothered in the slightest.
The IRS attached me for the $9,000 donation I gave to the
Conspiracy Trial. I had to do a speaking tour to pay the government! They are trying to set some example. Three IRS audits
in three years. Noah was always busy. Remember the bag of
heroin and the gun planted in my office.

Also, I've not won every case, as you've said, and the only
jury trials I've had have been lost. Not only have I not won
every case, I've actually jumped bail in southern cases before.
It was standard practice the system was so rigged. I pleaded
guilty to the Columbia charges, although innocent. I went to
jail in Chicago for FUCK on my forehead. Lots of demonstration busts led to fines and probations. In no way have I
"won" every case. The governmment has admitted in various
courts eight wiretaps on me. I'm sorry to lay out all this stuff
but I'm somewhat emotionally concerned right now.

I think stuff on the arresting cops will break.

I miss the kid something fierce, especially since I had a
vasectomy too. I think that's had some effect on my thinking
and besides I love him very much. I don't know what to tell
you. There's gotta be a strong psychosomatic component to

him all of a sudden being sick all the time. God honey, what can we do? We could never live together. My being hunted is too heavy a burden for you. The only way is if you got romantically off on the tension and adventure that it guarantees and I don't think you're romantically in love with me for that trip. I think you see me as your best friend, your "brother," your kid's father, but all that would tend to keep us apart. It's all too sensible and there's nothing sensible about wearing an amulet with cyanide and being somewhat on borrowed time.

I hope you go to Europe this summer. I wish you could see and meet people who are not New York thinkers—maybe even change your name and disappear with junior or without. Say for two months. Really try to make it on your own. Then maybe you'll see how meaningless all this struggle crap is. How lonely people are who "make it on their own." I hate to see you down and the kid sick. God. Do anything to correct the situation. Commit bigamy. Give the kid to an orphanage. Leave the country. Or join me. Better not. Oh, there would be less attention to the kid needed but, to use your words, you'd "have two kids to look after." Not that you ever said that to me but all our friends talk. If you're not into the romantic adventure then don't come. Don't ever come, even for a peek. I'm living life to its fullest. I'm determined to make a good thing out of this and grow in loads of ways. I fight boredom and mundane living with a manic ferocity that must be sick. I don't give a fuck. I want to die like I live, HIGH!

This letter keeps wiggling out of control. I don't know what I'm writing about since it's all between the lines, stuff that even I don't understand. In point of fact there is a difference between being friends and lovers. Everybody in the world knows that. If we were lovers we would be together. Let's face it. It's pretty easy to pull it off without being followed. It's pretty easy to preprogram junior or even dump him as Archie and Veronica suggested. They, by the way, are lovers and not friends. That's

why I have trouble digesting all your compliments. Maybe
you're right and I'm wrong. I'm under the spell of simplistic
rock lyrics and surrounded by simple people with simple needs.
Oh, I can buzz'em with an idea or two in a way that reaches
them and gets them to regard me as one who has information
they don't. But so. Sometimes I think it's just devilish.

God, if we were together we'd talk continuously. I'd want
to fuck every hour and you'd never be alone. I don't think that
excites you. Maybe what I'm saying is we probably should
separate spiritually as well as physically. God, I can't even
spell the word my hand trembles so. Love is all I can offer
and my presence. Obviously you want more in life, you want
fulfillment. I don't see how I can provide that. Here's the nut
of it: each good strong step I take you'd see as a threat.

Look, tell me how it works. I've met women before and after
who have incredible strength and beauty and live alone, even.
Very independent types. I look around me and I see loads of
women who are brave, courageous, alive, functioning and not
liberated to the extent that they could battle out their views in
group sessions. They are not trained to compete. I don't think
you have been either. If you were you'd be up before the kid.
You'd never relax. You'd rush the barricades with a ferocity
that comes from training continually for battle. I'll tell you
what competition is about. Black and blue hands for weeks so
they're tough enough to smash bricks.

God, when I was little, which I still am, I'd go totally ape-
shit over a sport. I'd spend twelve hours a day mastering techniques. Now probably everything was useless energy. I never
really seemed to be able to discipline myself to learn important stuff like typing or foreign languages or auto mechanics.
I'm trained to be quick-footed and quick-tongued. A flash in
the sky. I don't have the stamina for the long, grinding haul
of life. What's more, I don't even want it! I want to have fun,
fight, be free, fuck, feel, fall on my arse, fiddle with life's inner

workings. I don't want to BE CAREFUL. I don't want to grow up. I want to be ridiculously childish and I want a child for a playmate. A beautiful sweet curvy titted woman who's going to want to fuck me as much or more than I want to fuck her. "I believe in music, I believe in Love." Blind, emotional, sexual, compassionate love. Go your way, princess. You're too smart to cut the mustard with a macho maniac like me. You could take money, live in a foreign country, get a maid and write. You could rob a bank. You could take the kid's clothes off, your own too, stand in Times Square and scream that you demand a Socialist government that cares for the homeless. You could hook some schmuck with money. You could stop smoking dope and cigarettes. You could cut your sleeping in half. You could hitchhike to the Coast. I don't know, there's hundreds of things you could do. All I know is, Honey, I ain't got what you all want. The only way you're going to be free is to get legally divorced, change your name, and start anew.

Don't you see you're spinning rubber, toots. What a book title you laid out. You call that independence. It's like your life began when you met me. How could we ever be equals. I've written 140 pages and I'm not even through college yet. I thought your book should start at your birth, etc., but hey, I'm really honored to have turned you on to life. You did me to a great extent. Thanks. But don't come see me because I'm your goddamn guru or we're old friends. Only come 'cause you're in love with me. Because you wake up in the morning groping for another playmate to start the day and the best one you know is wasting his time writing forty-page letters and smashing bricks for little kids he thinks are his kids.

Night's coming. How can I write with such restrictions. No wonder no one ever wrote what it's like living under. I think we're moving toward equality slowly but surely. I think maybe my love for you is fading. I wish I could say what I feel. It's just changing. Maybe I'm just walling myself up against your loss of love. "Well, fuck her, it was fun while it lasted but what's new." All I want is your criticism on the project. After that I'll ask nothing.

You are the only person to ever raise the issue of "Ugh, another thing he wants me to do!" Even in the way you did it. You would not believe the offers, and the number getting off on helping. Oh, I know your feelings are really like all your friends who want to do everything but stay with the kid. I know. But still I have one rule going: If you don't get off on helping, don't. I helped people like this and loved it, in fact I was pissed when I wasn't asked to do more. That's true. There's something spiritually rewarding about aiding and abetting. It seems like classic good works. The simplistic do-gooder stuff that translates into any culture and time in history. Dig this! Last week I arranged for someone to get phony papers to leave the country. Details have to be left out. It was dangerous all right, but I really got off on the idea of help. It kept me going all week. I know I'm walking a tightrope. But goddamn it, fuck'em. I'm licking the sweat from my shoulder. It's all I've eaten today. Yum! Yum! So here I am giving you all sorts of errands, advice, wearing you down. You have to sort out the wheat from the chaff. DO YOU ACTUALLY THINK I CARE if you take the advice? You think I'm threatened if you don't? Babes, I *like* giving advice. The process I mean. Like that talk to Alvin, part of which you heard. It buzzes in my head still. Two things I could have said better. Everything I could do better. I want to be perfect when I die. I want to be happy. Every once in a while I replay speeches in my head given five years ago and come across a bump and polish it.

What a handicap. I try never to repeat myself but letters and tapes are lost, floating through the universe. I'm just frustrated hon.

I have to start saying good things about you. (1) You give me the best info I get. I have to hunt for it, but it's there. You are by far the best contact I have. Well-rounded, valuable, exciting. Slurp! Slurp! (2) You're walking a tightrope too, and want to have your cake and eat it too. I love and admire you for that. You are fighting hard for life. The fact that you should get up before junior and exercise for an hour each day is sort of like you advising me to learn how to type. Get it. And much of this letter is a reaction. Like an animal in some psych. experiment that's just been shocked.

This letter is draining me. You compel me to think in ways that only compel me to think more, not to figure out life's challenge. I guess this is my down letter that you cautioned against, a while back. Remember, "don't write down letters or it gets contagious." But two are lying on the floor next to my bed. And they represent a lot I flushed down the toilet. Everyone says you're doing remarkably well. I'm proud of you. Now what?

I'm broke and upset that I never laid the story of the bust out despite the risks. As soon as someone else is getting off on the work that needs to be done I can stop asking you to do anything. Right. You can go to Europe or travel for as long as you want. You can be totally free of me and my idiot requests. You already got a kid. Lots of people don't. Let'em in on the action. It's that simple. Zap——you're free.

Honey, WHAT IS THE MEANING OF LIFE?

> Your wounded comrade,
> Corpus Delecti

Newest fantasy of the kid and me: Dada is hiding in the woods. So junior will *parachute* into the woods with his *telescope* and look for him. When he finds him he will put on his cowboy hat and guns and will shoot "pow" the bad guys, and rescue Dada.

Funny, I complain a lot about the kid keeping me at home, but I'm beginning to see that the kid keeps me moral and serious and not so caught up in groupie celebrity social trash. Darling, I find I like to work. The times I am happiest are when I'm writing. But problems. I'm not doing the piece for *Viva*. Too personal, and I'd have no editorial control. I don't want to be ashamed every time I pass a newsstand. Still waiting to hear from *Redbook*.

The whole gang is broke too, but last night they chipped in for a sitter so I could join the dinner party farewell for Jesse, Penny and Leslie, who are leaving town for different destinations. We went to a restaurant in Chinatown where the nine of us sat around a huge table. The waiter gave us a box of fortune cookies and mine said, "Two people coming your way. The one with the darker hair loves you best."

I know it's true. That you love me more perhaps than anyone ever shall. And sometimes I think that no matter how crazy our life together would be, it would be more normal, more secure, than what we each experience now. Even if the three of us were living in poverty in one room, one of us could always take the kid to the park. I think back to our life at the Chelsea. Even though we were fighting, there were still good moments. I think even a drudge job would be more tolerable if I could come home at night to you and the kid. At least when

I got home we would have a life together instead of just loneliness and fear of the future. Then I think, if you go back to
him, to be the woman at his side, you'll have given up. You will
live and die by his side, your whole life nothing but a wife.

Other men seem bland compared to you. I've had an affair or
two but nothing earth shaking, nothing, as they say, to write
home about. Jealous. You should only have cause to be jealous.
I could use a little excitement. Maybe there are sexy, interesting men out there but I don't get out enough to meet'em. It's
not the most important thing, but it would be fun. I mean sex
is the dessert in life and I like sweets. I think more like a
man now; I only think of sex for relaxation and amusement,
like movies. Yet I'm not suited for promiscuity 'cause I don't
enjoy it unless there's passion, and I rarely feel that way about
people. It would be good for the kid if I had a boyfriend, a
male who was around a lot. Junior loves men and remembers
every one he meets. I hope I didn't goof by referring to sex, still
a delicate subject I guess. Only I figured, if *nothing*'s doing,
what can be bad to write?

I'm aging. By the time we meet I may look like your mother.
Big circles under my eyes. We can do the gigolo trip. What a
fantasy! We meet at some tropical seaside resort. I'm a wealthy
career woman and I come with my son. I meet a young, hand-
some guy who becomes my lover, forsaking his lithe beauties
for this faded Ava Gardner in menopause. If only the wealthy
part would come true . . . I would support you in style. New
tennis sneakers for all! And underwear from Bloomingdales.

I love you.

P.S. I'm glad you're sticking to morality.

Dear love,

Letters June 3 and 4 just arrived. I'm sorry I sent last letter. None of those things are that important I asked of you, believe me. It's really hard communicating with you over time lapses. We have to take that into account. You have to maybe accept the fact that something said in a letter has been rethought again and commented on in a subsequent letter that's been delayed. Things are going to go faster. I'm so alone. I can't think everything out, damn it! I need some feedback.

I'm really singing today. You must achieve your goals of success, please struggle with zeal. I want you to succeed more than to be together with you. Sincerely. Sometimes each of us acting alone is wrong but each correcting the other works fine. Once the project is over we can just write each other on feelings.

Yours in ecstasy,
Fanny Hill.

He said, in a low voice, looking down, his fleshy lips puckering, "I have no Daddy."

So I explained about the good guys and the bad guys and jail, and how we'll all be together when it's safe. I said, "Daddy had to hide so the bad guys don't hurt him, but he sends us letters, and he cries because he misses his boy so much."

He said you were Superman, and I agreed, suppressing my secret suspicion that you probably do resemble Clark Kent now. He also said you're a fireman wearing a firecoat and hat and boots. I agreed you might be one. A good disguise. He seemed reassured.

I better keep repeating that stuff, huh? Maybe tomorrow we'll make a tape and send it. I wish you could send him a letter with pictures on it, but I'm afraid he'll talk about it and want to take it to school, and that's no good.

He took a bath today, after much resistance and three weeks. He feels so especially cuddly. His skin is so smooth. He loves to hug and kiss and do tricks, balancing up in the air on my feet. I put him to bed without a diaper tonight for the first time. When he's hungry he'll say, "How about raisins?" "How about watermelon?" "How about yogurt?" If he gets yogurt he smears it on the dark wooden table and fingerpaints with it. He insists on cutting all his food himself, which he can't do.

Sometimes he pretends he's an Indian and shoots an imaginary arrow the way I showed him. He likes to pretend a lot. The other night he pretended there was a swimming pool in the kitchen and jumped into it from the kitchen chair. Then he "swam" across the floor into the living room, like a lizard. Tonight he licked my face and said, "Woof, woof, I'm a dog."

Then he asked me for a bone. A red bone, a yellow bone, a blue bone. Then he bared his teeth. "I'm a dinosaur." "Oh, I'm so scared. I'm scared of dinosaurs." He loves that. "I'm a monster. A monster crab." "Oh, I'm so scared of monster crabs."

Some mornings he comes bouncing into the living room, where I sleep, and gives me a big kiss. Then he watches TV until I wake up. He collects baseball cards for the "sugar gum" inside, which he swallows, although I tell him not to. He likes to sing songs he hears on TV. He knows three-quarters of the alphabet and can count to six sometimes.

You don't know cute until you've seen this one. And you will. If we play it right, he'll be able to handle the changes. I wish he could see and play with you tomorrow. I wish I could hop on a train . . . but they'd follow.

He's the most beautiful thing we've ever created. If you could only see him sleeping. The rosy cheeks, the long eyelashes. So skinny. Too skinny. When I reject him 'cause I'm busy he buries his head in my thigh and I can never resist patting that head. When he goes to sleep, sometimes he puts his arm around me in the most protective fashion.

Tonight he finally said, "You're my friend. My friend Anita." It was the nicest thing he's ever said to me. Even nicer than "I love you Mommy."

I want you to experience him too. Sharing his love will augment ours.

Dear Juliet!

"Death to the fascist insects that prey upon the people."
DO-WA-DO-WAH. DO-WA-DO-WAH.

I'm listening to SLA tapes in one ear, fifties rock music in the other and I'm rereading June 9 letter from you which I just got. It's incredible I can no longer match your canny mind and open heart. The story of you and junior wiped me out. I can't understand what you mean by you're making me angry with your letters and thoughts. Sometimes I think how far apart we are when you predict anger and none appears. Although I have gotten angry at other times.

I like your feelings toward kid. I would have liked you as a mother. You're so fucking smart and so brave. It's good that the kid keeps you moral. Immorality is the bottomless pit. Absolutely. It is not natural for you or me. It takes generations of breeding to develop someone who can be immoral with any sort of natural style. I envy no immoral person. Do you envy anyone? Immoral people envy others.

Something really strange has occurred in my life. I have been loved by women who don't even know who I am. Don't you think that's just insane? I'd like to really open up. I think we could write more about experiences and friends, in intimate detail and honesty. This is risky but good. I think about it all the time and can handle it at this end. You probably sense something's up from the June 4 letter. Since the day we parted, even before, when you said one night you didn't think you loved me anymore, I began preparing myself for accepting life without you. I went through excruciating torture. On a few

43

occasions I was pretty hurt by you. Something I was not only
totally unprepared for, but found incredibly hard to understand, except to tell myself "she's doing this so she can be free."
Anyway I felt I had hurt you sometimes too. So fair's fair.
About a week ago I started having fantasies and dreams about
other women. Can you imagine, for months on end almost since
the bust, I've only dreamed and thought of you. I mean I
practically saw no life worth living without you, and here you
were saying no. I almost died of a broken heart. At times I
didn't care if I lived or died, *not* because I was hunted but because of you. That's over. Definitely over. That's what I meant
about us being more equal.

I live alone, which is strange. I've been going steady for
twenty-three years! I see a lot of possibilities and quite frankly
I'm not pressing you to pack up and rush over here as you can
tell. Seems to me that's a lot better than my previous condition. I'm interested in two things: happiness and creativity.
And I'm going to arrange the whole fucking world to achieve
both, in that order. Oh right, I'm interested in not getting
caught, that's important. By the way, do you think you could
get jealous? How do you relate to me living with another
woman? We've never really broached the subject but to me it
seems inevitable that it's going to eventually happen.

I'll get right to the sex stuff. Yes, we have different attitudes.
First off, I'm not jealous of anything you do, but I'm really
curious. What do you mean "sex is not so important," you
"think more like a man now." You only think of sex as relaxation and amusement? Is that how men think? No wonder there
aren't too many interesting men around. Then a contradiction,
"I like passion, not just physical stuff." Good sex is interesting.
Don't relegate it to "relaxation." You sound like a tired businessman home from the office stopping off at the local massage
parlor. For one thing there's ego gratification in them thar
hills. There is danger. Always the risk of some form of rejec-

tion. There's the whole learning from the other what gives pleasure and simultaneously receiving pleasure. Working out a give and take. That's fun! Like when to be active, when passive. Using that little knowledge to examine all life. Active-passive is probably the big Yin-Yang, don't you think? If you're active constantly in sex you miss half the sensations, and never learn what the other knows. Dancing is like that. It's tough for the male to learn how to follow the woman's movements and respond to them, and few women feel confident enough to lead. But *some* do, and everything's gonna change.

Rereading letter I'm interested in "sex is the dessert of life." Hmmmmmmmmmmm mmmmmm. I guess so. No, I can't accept that. Oh, it's O.K., but why dichotomies? Is life spread out before us like a five-, six-, seven-course meal? Waiter, oh waiter. Let's see, we're very hungry. Let's start with some Interesting Ideas for appetizers, then move on to Soupe des Arts, and for the main course she'll have a Child and I'd like an Interesting Job. Now we'll follow that with a Big Cause, preferably one we can share, and we'll wash it down with some Mechanical Conveniences, top it off with a Tropical Beach and now for dessert WANNA FUCK? I don't know. My stomach's usually too full for dessert.

A faded Ava Gardner and a beachboy in new sneakers! I like that! I'm into beautiful women, not pretty girls. I definitely do not prefer young women and I'm pretty interested in this because most men definitely do. I have no Lolita fantasies. Well, not entirely. There was this young girl I used to see around the neighborhood. No, nothing really. Not like other men have. There's not much to learn. You can't get into the give and take much. All the women I go with are in their thirties. I'd like to tell you about two but only if you can get interested. I remember once I started to tell you an interesting sexual experience and you cut me off with, "God, I got my own problems, I couldn't give a shit about that."

Yes, Ava Gardner would be very nice. She was always faded, wasn't she? I guess I only knew her as an older actress. I can't think of "growing up with Ava." She was always already there!! You really would support me? GIGGLE GIGGLE. I love you dollie.

Oh, I forgot.

"Death to the fascist insects that prey upon the people and all power to the DDT of the proletariat class."

Don Q. Hotty

The enclosed quote from the *New York Review of Books* chilled me. Is it wrong to share fear?

When the military searched a home in Las Barrancas, Santiago, the wife apparently complained it was the third such search and wouldn't they please leave her family in peace. As the military departed, they said to the little boy outside, "So long, kid, you won't be seeing us around anymore." The child, surprised, inquired, "You mean you found my Daddy hiding in the roof?" The military reentered the house, brought the father downstairs and shot him in front of his family.

Darling:

I'm ashamed to write you so many down letters. I want to write but most of my activities are so mundane and depressing.

Like today. I applied for welfare. I'm tempted not to dwell on this because I don't want to depress you. The whole subject brings me down. Even though I'm super-sophisticated and entertain visions of a society where everything is free, I guess on some level I still believe applying for welfare is an admission of failure. That's why I've postponed doing it for so long. For the past two months the kid and I have been living on borrowed money. If I get an article assignment I can always get off, but going to welfare means I haven't made it.

I dreaded this day. You have to be on line by 7:30 A.M. to get into the welfare center, so I arranged for my friend Leah's daughter, Monica, to babysit. Kiddo still has a cough and I didn't dig the idea of waking him early and making him wait in line with me.

People advised me to wear my oldest clothes so I inspected the closet carefully this morning. The odd thing is, I ended up putting on the same clothes I wear every day. All my clothes date from the sixties and they are becoming rags with karma.

In my usual morning daze I subway up to the welfare center which is located, of all places, on Park Avenue and 28th Street. When I arrive, there are only four adults ahead of me, plus numerous children. There is no place to sit since we are in a hallway with a cop guarding the elevator. I knew most of the day would be spent waiting so I take out my book and lean against the wall. The book is *The Call Girls* by Arthur Koestler.

48

The title attracted me, but the book is really about the professional intellectuals who travel the world conference circuit, repeating the same ideas at every world-crisis junket they are invited to. It's a weird book to read in these surroundings. My mind is floating in the Swiss Alps with the bickering nuclear physicists and biologists while my body is, well, down there in the nitty gritty of enameled hallways and bawling children.

At 9 A.M. the elevator door opened and I was in the first batch to arrive at Applications. I waited there two hours but at least there were seats. People come prepared to sit for hours, everyone seems resigned to it. I was the only white person I saw and I wondered if that would work against me.

The receptionist was cold and skeptical. She asked me where my husband was. I said he had left us and was a fugitive. "What do you mean?" she said. "He's wanted by the law. He was arrested and he jumped bail." "What was he arrested for?" I kept it simple, "Drugs." "Ah." Yes, now she understood. She nodded quickly and got some papers out of a drawer. No more questions, the first hurdle had been passed. The key word was "drugs." I knew she figured you were a junkie, but I let it pass. She gave me an eleven-page application form and a list of items to bring in for documentation, plus some pamphlets that say nothing. I have to come back next week to file the application, which looks like a lulu. More intimidating than any I've seen.

I'll get out of this funk. In fact I took the kid to the park this afternoon to forget the morning. The problem of supporting us is a difficult one, but I didn't rise to the occasion. I will never regret not doing that *Viva* piece for a grand.

By the way, I reread your section on welfare in *Steal This Book* and should tell you that things have changed. It's not such a breeze to get on anymore. They require a lot of documentation: passports, birth certificates, income tax returns, social security cards, marriage licenses, even.

Can you believe I still have our marriage license. It never fails to surprise me that we actually have one, and now, finally, there is some use for it. The first marriage license issued in the state to the NeoAmerican Church! Did I ever tell you how nice you were to participate in that Jewish ceremony for my parents? My mother always refers to our anniversary as that date, although we use the date of the Central Park wedding [June 10]. There was also that Indian sitar ceremony Linn and Marty arranged, and the first time we took acid together. We called the trip our Lower East Side Honeymoon. That was when we kissed and I saw slot-machine cherries, bananas, pineapples and pears tumble before my eyes. I told you about it then, and years later when we were discussing sex you used it to conclude that women had more placid sex fantasies than men. You said I dreamed of vegetables!

I hope I get on welfare. I have thirty dollars in the drawer.

So, so far I haven't seen an overnight success. How can anyone be judged in terms of money? God, I just want to do what I want to do. Why is that so difficult? I want to sit in a corner and write. I want to work at something I believe in.

I WANT THE TIME OF MY LIFE.

"a lifetime burning in every moment"

love,
your old flame

I know this little kid same age as junior who adopts me as his "new daddy." I don't want him, I want junior. The kid stuff drives me to tears. I just sent a few drawings to him as you suggested. Sent them days before even. We are on the same wavelength. We feel exactly the same. I'm sure of it. I have feelings of unworthiness in our relationship, though, that I have to deal with. My manhood is definitely jolted by the idea of being an appendage to your strength. Hiding up on the roof even. Like some political paraplegic. After all, my most creative act is staying alive. That's not really Gunga Din Superstar stuff worthy of your flash! Nothing comes out of the pen right. Maybe your successes are a threat? God, all this thinking gets so circular.

How can you even ask, "Is it wrong to share fears?" What do you want to share—Wonderbread sandwiches for lunch?

I have no idea how we can all be together because kid is so unpredictable. There would have to be a period of adjustment where we could be isolated from the danger of mistakes. Do you think *you* could hack isolation? Of course the kid could and I'm sure I could. You're the question mark here. You see the problem of what happens if we don't make it and you go back to N.Y. and that world with the kid. He would talk about where his daddy is, and he would not want to leave me again. And of course I'd have to change my spots rapidly, maybe even appearance. That's why slow is best.

I'm pretty certain my personality is exactly the same although way back in the corner of my mind sits a little "me" that's unsure of the future, a little "me" that's been belted once too often by life, that doubts the past, that longs for death, whose legs are not as strong as they once were, and feels his talent is gone, the times are run out and he should learn the big lesson of life—nothing comes easy. It's just a little me but it's the one that wakes me up at night. The Failure. But then, of course, I'm really strong and getting along so well, and I wonder how others would function and, well, I accept myself.

True, sometimes I'm not interested in what you say. I apologize to you. I'm a performer so I spend a lot of time in my mind studying my lines. I do that to everyone. You the least. I'm a bragger, a show-off, an exhibitionist. That whole symdrome. If anything, I've gotten worse since you saw me. Although the act's improved a bit since there's this huge backdrop, LIFE OR DEATH, added to the play.

Some day down the future road we'll just have to get together and sniff each other out and try to do what's right. There's no second-guessing this stuff. You have to prove things to yourself which you don't seem to have done yet. I, too, have to prove things to myself. They are different things. Mine are not as big as yours right now.

Of course I'm free to make up my whole life within limits. I can walk out the door, can move from city to city, follow my whims. I have acquaintances you would never believe, and I can get somewhat off on lower-level-thinking humans in a way I doubt you could. Lots of this is male freedom versus female. The world out there from the gutter of the worst slums to fashionable country clubs, from pool halls to intellectual salons, to sports, to the streets alone. I am not afraid of the world. I don't know how a woman can come down the same road. I watch the lone woman sitting on the bus late at night. She has to bury her face in the magazine, for to look around her eyes might linger too long on the face of one of the lonesome men and he might think it's a come-on. And he might approach, or worse "attack"; neither of which she can ever do, of course.

The kid would love it here. Unquestionably a good deal for junior. You—I can't answer, you'll have to come and look real hard. There are great frustrations and to really get off you have to change considerably—the more the better. The *change* is the best part. I have no idea how long the infatuation lasts. This letter sems to be the other side of the June 4 letter which tells you to forget me and go marry someone else. That's the way the schizoids split, I guess.

In November or December we'll be together and if we're determined to live together we'll make it work. You got four more months to get your act in shape! Can't wait to tell you everything.

Today is July 4. Our apartment sounded like a battle zone in Vietnam. The only window in the living room overlooks a cement playground which tonight was a minefield of fire-crackers. Sometimes the boom-booms lasted for ten minutes straight; sometimes everything in the apartment shook as though an atomic bomb had just dropped on 57th Street and we were getting the first reverberations. The kid was crying and scream-ing "stop" at the sounds, and I didn't know what to do. It was his bedtime and he wanted to go to sleep but there was no relief from the explosive noise. I kept looking out the window to see where it was all coming from but all I could see were the sparks from firecrackers and occasional flashes of lightning. I stuffed cotton in our ears but that didn't work. I held the kid for a long time, then tried to get him interested in his cow-boy gun (he wouldn't have to say "POW" tonight) without much success. Just as I squat to kill a cockroach on the floor, lightning flashes and I look up, and lo and behold, there are fireworks in the sky! That's what the big booms were. The trick is that you can only see them out of the window by lying on the floor. If you stand and look out, buildings block the view of the sky above Houston Street, where they're coming from. So I put pillows on the floor and we spent the rest of the evening lying there watching the fireworks. I think I liked them even more than the kid. My favorites are always the orange ones which turn into wiggly fishes. I feel there is a moral here somewhere. Look Up and Live? A patch of blue . . .? Every cockroach has a silver lining?

The kid's asleep now and the hubub has died down, I hope, for another year. My mother's in town and will be taking junior to visit your mother in Massachusetts in a few days. Saturday we're having a big birthday party for him in Leslie's loft. Mother's coming over tomorrow night so I can go to Leslie's to bake the cakes which will be angel-chiffon with whipped cream, blueberries and strawberries. The loft is decorated already with red, white and blue streamers. Leslie's been paying for everything because I'm waiting for my welfare check. She's terrific. She's giving the kid the best present of all: his first birthday party. The kid is in ecstasy and keeps announcing to anyone in listening distance, "I'm three years old." I invited all the children, teachers and parents from his daycare center, in addition to our friends and Leslie's. I think whoever is in the city will come. There's not much else to do here. It's going to be a long, muggy weekend.

Our friends have been so good to me and junior. Without them I would feel so alone. I tell them I love you. Ah, my dear, you are the most fascinating one in the world to me. How often I try to picture your face. My mind becomes a slide machine and I imagine you in my favorite attitudes. Strangely, a lot of them are childish yous, little-boy yous. I always was a sucker for cute.

Trains are dying a sad death. Too bad. Most romantic form of travel. Full of mystery and intrigue. Imagine this small group of travelers, outlaw fugitives, totally apart from anyone else on the train, yet ham acting the whole time and every once in a while giggling. Like, I just had drinks with a group of men headed for sailfishing, which is the ultimate Pig Sport. You know, catch the big fish (uneatable) and plaster it on your den wall. The conversation was strange.

I'm really missing a companion and if we don't get hitched soon I'm thinking of marrying someone else. No shit. I've had the idea for a few days now. First I got this idea about polygamy, then I keep asking myself, well, why is polygamy illegal? I mean, who the hell's business is it? Then I'm thinking, hey, it's the perfect solution to the divorce problem and can express a new consciousness. Yes, it's time we had a new look at polygamy. Anyways, I've been looking around for interesting little laws to break and up pops the big P. Naturally it's for both sexes. I mean, say we just can't hack it together for who knows what reasons and yet still want to say what we feel, that we're in love, and then some other people pop along down life's road. I think it's O.K. to marry them. Hey, for me it's an extra piece of I.D., for you it could be a court battle. You must be somewhat up on the law 'cause I remember once when I asked you about how we could work out a divorce if I was John Doe in a few months and you said, in straight talk, "After five years we are legally divorced." I was so taken aback by your answer I just let it pass. I figured someone slipped you the info. I couldn't picture you climbing through lawbooks to find the answer.

I think the thought started bubbling when I read this story about one of those English rogues who robbed a British train of eleven million dollars and got away, and a few months ago turned up in Brazil where he just got a Brazilian pregnant. His wife in England said she loved him but would give him a quick divorce because there was a Brazilian law that the father of a Brazilian kid can't be extradited. I think that's how it goes. The story said Brazil would not send him back. It may be a money payoff too. I'd be damned if I'd trust Brazilian law, and they sure as hell aren't about to trust me there, even with seven Brazilian wives. And the vasectomy cuts down the kid route.

But then I got to thinking how funny it would be to be a real live Bigamist and was sort of pissed I wasn't in big-time love enough with another woman and above ground to do it. Although it should really be done by a woman since that's really unique and a great political and constitutional fight. Imagine that's the best political idea I've had in months and I'm real excited 'cause my brains are getting rusty and I keep wondering what happens when you never have an original thought and I guess that's when you take up sailfishing.

I'm more confident we can stay friends than lovers. I cannot conceive of any situation that would destroy that. Can you? There is some bond between us that can never change, it's frozen in time and space. We have burned buildings together, made love in Venice, robbed together, been in adjoining cells, borne a child out of deepest love, we have shared ecstasy and agony with such good feelings toward each other that it could only change if one or both of us went crazy—got badly beaten by life and well, it ain't happened yet. . . .

He kept dreaming that someday he'd be a star
(a superstar but he didn't get far).
But he sure found out the hard way
dreams don't always come true

Oh no.
So he pawned all his hopes and
even sold his old car.
Bought a one-way ticket back to the life he once knew.
Oh yes he did. He said he would.
Oh yes he did. He said he would.

Now he's leavin on that midnight train to Georgia.
Said he's going back to find
a simpler place in time.

I'm gonna be with him on that midnight train to Georgia.
I'd rather live in his world than be without him in mine.

(my world, his world, our world, mine and his alone)

I've got to go
I've got to go
I've got to go . . .

Just got your June 27 letter. In November or December I'll
go. Our song always cheers me even when it makes me cry.
But I have to be honest, that line "I'd rather live in his world"
bothers me. It's not what I chose to do. What's love babes?
I say I love you and I know it's true even if we were together
and quarreling. I'm wondering if it would be better for me to

58

visit without the child, initially. That way he won't have to go through so many readjustments so fast, and we would have no excuses for not getting along. I know you want to see him, but maybe such a quickie wouldn't be good for him or you. I don't know, maybe it would be cruel to deny you even his brief presence.

I am amazed that you should ever consider yourself a failure, but it's reassuring to know that you, too, have moments of doubt. Don't be down, toots. If I was beside you I would curl around you and protect you from all bad dreams. Just remember, you're Free. This morning I was thinking how that means everything.

O.K. Cheer-up Time. Rest Break. Fifteen minutes of Sex Discussion coming up. Been meaning to reply to you for days. You are hilarious. You are devasting. What can I say? We're at different places, that's all. See, most women plan their lives around men, usually the source of sex. Their self-image depends on ego-gratification from the affection of men. That is not a healthy state. Besides, I have responsibilities. I'm trying to learn about gratification from achievement. A new trip. So I compartmentalize my life and I push sex into a corner where it only means relief from tension, relaxation, escape from the daily grind. The tired businessman's trip. It's actually a relief to be immune from the pangs of love, the exhausting illusions of Romance. I'm having friendships with men I've never had before because neither of us are preoccupied with love or possession. We value the friendship and want to be liked for who we really are, so we're honest. Although I don't get out much, I did have a boyfriend about a month ago. We saw each other regularly for two months and then it just sort of dissolved through mutual boredom or because we weren't in love. I had called him first, by the way, something I'm real proud of. We like each other and are still friends. Maybe the thing I enjoyed most about the relationship was that we weren't in love.

I'm going to run a few quotes that might trigger you to read *Notes from the Underground* which I don't think you have and would really enjoy. For me it's the second time and it's triggering all sorts of clickings in my pinball head. It is word-for-word probably the most thought-provoking book I've ever read. Dostoevsky is such a genius of a writer. He works so hard behind the scenes to say something so provokingly simple. I think he took his whole life and jammed it into his work. He worked incredibly hard. Reading half the night, taking hundreds of pages of notes for every two or three he wrote. And just flooding the world with masterpieces. I'm fascinated by his style because I don't think he was that interesting a person.

The book *Notes* is a novel, and if you haven't read it it's not what you think. Underground is human loneliness or a sort of intellectual, vacuum-packed cocoon. "Conscious inertia" as Dostoevsky says. It's an anonymous man writing a critique of rationalism, laying bare more than any other D's mental agility. I have trouble tuning in on much of his thinking—suffering to purge guilt, certain negativistic thinking and don't see my underground in any way like his. In fact, the opposite really, but listen: "I invented adventures for myself and made up a life so as at least to live in some way." "Oh gentlemen I consider myself an intelligent man only because all my life I have been able neither to begin nor finish anything." He has this great passage on seeking a career or an identity as anything, even a "sluggard," and tells about a man he knew who only prided himself on his judgment of Lafitte wines and went to his death not just tranquilly but triumphantly.

It doesn't matter how much you or I agree with stuff in

this gem, there's something for everyone in it. God, what a writer. Another favorite of mine is *Journey to Ixtlan,* Castaneda's best book. I wonder how long his books will last because I don't think the institutional critics take him too seriously, 'cause he's having this sort of hippie-dippy success. Sort of like the Andy Warhol of Mysticism. But I like him fine in the same way I like Warhol and for me the book says a lot. Don Juan is such a hot shit of a sorcerer. This and the Dostoevsky book are terrific together. A great double bill. Don Juan is such a tower of strength compared to Dostoevsky's intellectual underground. Such great fun to hang out with, and Castaneda tells the story terrifically (and plays the media hype surrounding it). He has a perfect balance of wit and wisdom, of giving and receiving, of content and form. He has created the sensation that he, the scientific inquirer, has changed his life. A very neat trick indeed. Some people say Don Juan's made up. Not any more than Socrates was made up by Plato, I think. There's a nice chemistry that happens when a learning relationship clicks into time and place. When the student-teacher roles can continuously be revolving so that who's the teacher? Who's the student? Questions become a waste of time then. I think that's LOVE. What do you think? Student!

I've been gathering material the past few days for an article about poor women. There is no guarantee I can get it published but it's something I want to do.

I just got back from Brooklyn where I went to talk with some welfare recipients. My head is buzzing and I feel like crying because all my worst suspicions are true. Poor women with children abound in the thousands, nay, the millions. Their lives are miserable. I wouldn't be so frightened if it was not a possibility for me. The situation of women alone with children has not changed really since the beginning of recorded history! In every civilization women have been stuck with the children and forgotten; they are the poorest of the poor. Welfare is nothing but a modern equivalent of the poorhouse. It keeps us off the streets. Without welfare New York would be worse than Calcutta. Some people think welfare prevents revolution because without it there would be more grabbing. They say it's a sop to keep the dissatisfied quiet. Next week I'm interviewing an old leader of the welfare-rights movement. I have a lot of questions for her.

I'm confused. The women's movement isn't focusing on what needs to be done. I realize how absurd their preoccupations are when I see masses and masses of truly oppressed women that they are not reaching or helping. How can any woman be free while her sisters constitute the majority of the poor? How can the merits or demerits of prostitution be discussed at forums without any reference to the economic conditions which force women into prostitution? How can NOW have their big conference on sexuality? Sex is a luxury for women who can't even get out of the house. If you can't get out of the house it doesn't matter if you prefer stray dogs. Oh, if it weren't for the women's movement I might not even have these thoughts, so I don't really want to put it down. But I see how little has changed and how vast are the problems and it makes me rethink ideas about social change.

What is my role, what part can I, so recently from the middle class, play? The women suffering most are black and Puerto Rican, and it was black women who led the struggle for welfare rights in the sixties. Whites on welfare outnumber blacks, however, in national statistics. The point is that any woman, unless she's inherited wealth, can end up in this situation if she leaves her husband. For a woman with children the ultimate risk of personal liberation is poverty. Without free daycare and a guaranteed income women will never be equal, no matter how much discussion there is about the clitoris or the matriarchy or women's football teams or women's banks. Sure the consciousness is important, all those subtle male-female battles you and I fight out, but that stuff becomes neurotic bullshit compared to the physical deprivations millions suffer, with no hope of relief, because of their sex.

I want to write about all this. I feel bad because I don't know enough yet, and maybe I won't have enough time before the money runs out to learn everything I need to know. What a fucking jungle out there. Capitalism. Reform is like a Band-Aid. If you care about redistribution of wealth you have to think about radical change, change at the roots, revolution. I've led such a sheltered life, never having to struggle for survival. What an eyeopener.

Luv,

I awoke early with a hangover, having spent last night with
the Indian Princess. I took her out to the fanciest night club in
town. It was really strange. First, you know how we both feel
real uncomfortable in places like that, right? Well, after a drink
or two I'm getting into the place and really marveling about
how it's not done bad and it's very well designed. Then the
show begins and there's a rock group and a singer comedian,
who looks like Milton Berle with a long-haired wig on. And
they are all, I have to admit, pretty good. The guy makes me
laugh several times and I'm clapping like everyone else in the
club. They're off and the dance band comes on and Indian
Princess and I are dancing. Now you know how I love dancing
and I've gotten much better because of all this body concentra-
tion I've been into. Now Princess is really a surprise dancer. I
want to tell you a little more about her because in a way she's
kind of the heroine to this little chapter of my life and her life
says something about problems women face. She comes from
a strict, rich, old-fashioned family. When she was little the
women ate after the men were through, and although her family
has lots of money it's only passed on to the male heirs so she's
out of the gelt although she has a truly aristocratic manner
about her. She is nothing though like the rich we know. She's
led the life of a convent nun. At twenty-one she got married
to an engineer, married she said so she could get out of
the house. If you were married you could walk out the front
door. If you took a powder out the back it was bye-bye forever.
She realized after a year she didn't love her husband, and

years of isolation followed. They had two kids. After eight years of marriage he told her he had a girlfriend and wanted a divorce. Divorce to her was a word, even though she was miserable, like cancer. She even tried to kill herself by ripping open her wrists with a sharp pin. She got a job after that as a secretary but it was death, afraid of all men until she met me.

It was for us both a matter of convenience. We both lived alone. She had a car. I've got a license but rarely drive because getting pinched or in an accident would present some problems. I was a companion for her because she wanted to go places but was afraid to go alone. (This is not N.Y. City.) Naturally she had no women friends. Married ones thought she'd vamp, and besides women, and men too, for that matter, are not educated in how to make friends of the same sex.

At first the relationship took on pretty comic proportions. Lots of which are tough to detail. But she's not yet divorced although at first she told me she was. On the second or third date. And "date" is the right word. Like I think of the last couple hundred women I've "gone out with"—we've fucked on the first date. I can't think when it didn't happen. Anyway we're going through this whole adolescent scene and I'm playing along. I met her on this corner and we're going for dinner one night when she says, "Jump in fast my husband's following us," and I'm a little stunned because to me she's "divorced" already. I don't see another car so I think she's a little off her trolley but get in and she's racing all around and finally we end up at this nice French restaurant I'm into trying. She's all excited about being there. See, her old man never took her out to nice places, only places with the children on weekends and she was in a cocoon like you can't begin to imagine. So we're just getting through the snails when in pops HUBBY!!! And she sees him coming and all of a sudden he's at the table and she introduces us and we've got the same first name! At least the name I was using was the same as his. So it's "Frank, I'd like you to meet Frank," (which were not the names), and before I can say Frank this guy says, "Pleased to meet you," and sticks his hand out to shake and I'm shaking it and he says to her, "I'll be over Sunday to take the kids out," and leaves. Next comes the salad and Indian Princess is playing it very quiet and finally breaks the ice and says "I don't blame you if you never want to see me again." And I said, "No, it was getting too interesting." I really cussed out the hubby for doing such a mean thing and told her to tell him that if he pulled it again I'd fight him, and I meant it. She said he probably was trying to show she was going out with men or something and then not have to pay alimony. I told her to get a woman lawyer, who had been divorced, the next day. It was the best advice I ever gave anyone but she didn't, not for months. She still thinks, remember, that she got leprosy and will be cursed for life as a divorced woman. Then I realize why all the secret meetings.

Now our big balling scene (after necking in the car for two more weeks) is coming up and we meet *separately* at this hotel. Now I'm all dressed up, right, and arrive early and make the room arrangements and say wifey's coming along soon, just went to get some magazines. So pretty soon she comes driving along wearing huge dark glasses and a scarf. Now she's attractive. She's not the sort to stop traffic but if you were sitting near her and began studying her you'd soon be struck by this incredibly classic look to her features and you'd have this irresistible urge to touch her cheek.

Anyways—so she enters the room and I'm all into let's order dinner and everything and she lunges at me and throws me on the bed and she's really going into her act. Ah well . . . and I'm not even that horny (honest). So naturally I've got to close the blinds (although the only way you could see us is with a helicopter) and put the lights out and soon we're under covers and thumping away. After a minute or so there's this knocking at the door and I yell out that we're busy, go away, and then we wait and there's this coughing and she says it's her husband's cough and I'm really getting pretty pissed. I wrap a towel around me and grab this bottle and yank the door open ready to conk the bastard on the head. YANK! "Get the hell out of here," I yell. And just as I yell it the towel falls off and I'm standing there stark-naked staring dumbfounded at this startled bellhop. Who runs away. I call the desk and ask what's up and soon the bellhop's back with the assistant manager and it's just that they want their money up front cause they don't think we're this nice married couple like it says on the register.

That was really the only time we spent the whole night together and it kept going on and on like that the whole night. We balled about once a week and it was O.K. because I never pushed for any artistry or experimentation and she, I don't think, knew any. She was interesting though and I just kept marveling at the things she *did* know rather than being critical.

We got to like each other a lot and I don't think she loved me, it's just that she didn't really know the word for friend. I took her to lots of strange places. Like wrestling matches and a baseball game and these flea-bitten clubs filled with whores and knife fighters. (She had no notion of the word *slumming* nor do I for that matter.) And I used to cook for her, which threw her into absolute hysteria, and sometimes we took her kids out. Which she thought was very kind and it was, but I knew the problem and was into being her friend. Once I got her to try pot and it was really weird. She went into a strange orbit. O.D.'d and threw up. I never suggested it again. If she got too drunk I'd drive her home and walk back two miles or take a cab or bus once I knew she was safe.

Once we were in a supermarket and she was looking for a good book to read and picked up something by Irving Wallace from a rack next to copies of *Woodstock Nation*.* And I sort

* Abbie's second book.

of steered her away from the hot spot saying, "I know him, we met in London once." And it wasn't even a lie really because I've met him lots of places. Remember I'm this really sophisticated man of the world in this relationship. She, by the way, is far from being a dum-dum. Get this. She got a craving for Russian literature a few years ago and taught herself how to read and speak Russian. By herself! An Indian who speaks Russian to God knows who! Her great dream is to go to Moscow some day. I don't think it'll come true.

So here we are on our last night and we're in this extremely fancy club and we go to dance. Now she's a terrific dancer, but only of a certain type naturally having it all bottled up. When she dances she says with her body, "I am a leaf and you are the wind. Do with me what you will." And she is very light and floats in my arms which are very protective. And I can do all these intricate, slow, graceful maneuvers with her. Very Rudolph Valentino, exaggerated dips and arrests building into stylized twirls and culminating in a sort of reverse dip with me on one knee and her body draped backward over my other bent knee. WOW! I have no idea where I picked up this silly stuff but obviously I'm not having a bad time stepping on all my feet. (I'm really laughing out loud writing this stuff. But I'm interested in my dancing ability solely because I don't have any rhythm. So it's really more a puzzlement than a bragging thing.)

Remember I told you how she has this schizo thing like some Indian devil that comes out when she's drunk, her being the most reserved, polite little thing you could imagine when sober. So she takes off her shoes and says she prefers to dance barefoot like her ancestors—which I smile at and really think has a lot of class like she could actually be capable of passing into the international glamour world with some coaching. She has such a natural hidden flair for carrying on. So we're dancing and drinking and both pretty smashed although

I always play the Great Protector, you know, the one who says "enough." And as soon as she starts into this war dance and yelling these bloodcurdling shrieks throwing the whole place into chaos I grab her arm and say, "ENOUGH!" At which point she goes into her kicking me in the shins and "I'm jumping out the window" routine. And I do the over-the-shoulder "the lady's had a little too much to drink" number and carry her out of the place. A half-hour later she's calmed down and we're rolling in the grass of a park and she's pretty sad to see me go, but accepts this crazy excuse I've given her and sort of expects me back. And I'm tempted to tell her just sort of to see what will happen and maybe have another ally but decide not to and feel very proud. She's actually very strong and headed in a good direction and her flip-outs only come when she's drunk and possibly only with someone like me who plays a very strong, kind, role . . . and I say simply and slowly, "I'm not free." And we do goodbyes and good lucks at 4 A.M.

(By the by this is not, repeat, not the woman I mentioned in passing with whom I said I was infatuated. That's another—much more interesting and mysterious story. It's a story unfolding. It's the story of an affair with the Sphinx,* and when I get time and another pen I'll tell it.)

Is it O.K. to tell you stories like this about women? I think so, but I think it's polite to ask. So—now it's midafternoon. I awoke early this morning to do chores and returned to bed to rest before changing my spots for good late tonight. I packed, checked the place for telltale stains, you know. Being careful because I'm the sort of one who hides things and can't remember where later, which is not your best act when you're a fug (not pronounced like the old Fugs group but like the musical arrangement, how is that spelled, hon? Fugue?). So I'm lying

---

* The Sphinx is the same person who will later be called Angel.

in bed trying to go to sleep and I can't hypnotize myself and I try the fingers pressed in the acupuncture pressure points in your ears which Doctor Steve taught me—and I blank out and fall into a deep, peaceful sleep. I have some incredible dreams about designing different advertisements for products and am awakened by some loud noises and am annoyed I can't remember the dreams too well. I do some stretching exercises and get this idea to write a complete critique of *Casablanca* as counterrevolutionary Art and I'm plotting all the themes in my head, really onto things about Heroes and America and Sexual Roles, and so I pick up the pad and write you this letter instead. I mean I really got discipline, huh? I mean I'm such a lazy writer I write lying down. Hemingway wrote standing up and wouldn't fuck before he wrote, feeling it drained him. I mean actually who *wants* to be a Writer?

My bags are packed. Soon I will be in a new Zone and Head.

> Your ardent admirer and constant companion,
> Gulliver

I met Affeni Shakur today. What an up. She is vibrant, beautiful, wise with experience. We talked about our children a lot and the heavy history behind each. Did you know she named her son Tupac Amaru, after the last Inca prince who rebelled against the Spaniards? We had considered naming america that. Tupac's the same age. She says she tells Tupac that he began his life in jail because he should know and understand the history of his people. She said people will come down heavy on our sons because of who they are and they must learn the truth from the beginning in order to grow up strong.

The kid's been gone five days now and I've been traveling around the city, feeling terrific. Seeing Tupac reminded me of him, though. I do miss him a little.

Sex. You have terrific views and a great attitude. I liked reading all your experiences and am not in any ways jealous. In fact quite the opposite because it's *me* that's got the complicated affair going. The Sphinx, I mean, and there's a small chance I might tumble here and I'm not sure how to write about her to you because I'm not sure of all my feelings about what's possible and where everything and everyone is headed. I think I'll have a better insight by the time we meet. I should say that she's good for me and good for us. I'm just unsure about how to write you about another woman I obviously care about. It'd make great reading but well, obviously I've already told you but I'll need some signal from you about proceeding in this sensitive area.

Don't compare yourself to Ingrid Bergman in *Casablanca*. She's the Loser in the movie (I should have thought that through more before comparing her to you). She's just a pretty face with a tear in her eye. She's got no brain and less will. She's not even allowed to decide her future—Bogart decides it for her. Bogart's not my hero, he's a type of hero, the one who responds to a personal code but that's selfish in the end. Laszlo is a hero who responds *to the needs of the times*. Bogart's only greatness is recognizing that Laszlo's operating on a higher level than himself and in that realization commits a revolutionary act. It's no wonder that hip America, which glorifies the cut of rugged individualism, finds Bogart as its all-time hero. Superman in Woody Allen's Walter Mitty world. Allen's the funniest guy in the U.S. I love everything he does. But it's no wonder he once confessed to Jerry Rubin, "My life's nothing. All I do is entertain drunken conventioneers in Las Vegas.

At least you are trying to change the world." Woody's greatest whipping himself. Can you see a Chinese Woody Allen? I can't. Now all our educated friends are going to respond, "That's China's fault." I don't think so. It's not China that's spent thirteen years on the analyst's couch, it's Woody. Of course, I suppose it's asking too much to ask that revolutionary heroes be created in a country that is counterrevolutionary. The most one can hope for are rebels like Yossarian, like Lenny Bruce, like Bonnie and Clyde, and persons like Bogie and Mae West who "don't take no shit from no one." Revolutionary heroes take a lot of shit. They know they are used and use people all the time. You probably think I'm one. I'm not though. I'm a rebel, but I could be one of the first rebels who knew the difference and understood the part about "the needs of the time" being the crucial factor, not heroism in and of itself. Sure bravery is a nice quality—just like being for everything "good and beautiful." But let's just push everything further. Like consider Benefits for Chilean Refugees and how easy it is and defense funds and all that. It's good works; but guitar strumming, with tears glistening in the clear purism of Joanie's call for Peace and Love and goody-goody, is so fucking easy.

I think civil war is about to break out in Argentina. I think it could turn into our Spanish Civil War. What do you think? Argentina is a crucial country. Brazil and the Chilean junta would have to move. Argentina has a lot of natural resources. It's not a throw-away country and it's up for grabs. I'd like to know Joan Baez's views on Argentina rather than hear her cry tears for Chile in her next album. Maybe that's too tough. I'm not different from Joanie. We hung around Harvard Square together. We sat in the same coffee houses and nodded in rhythm to Pete Seeger. We're all children of our times. I'm asking myself as much as her or anyone else. How come we're so good at shedding tears for the dead and slow when it comes to slipping guns to the living? Because we're pacifists, basically. Well, the military in Argentina is about to wash the streets of Buenos Aires with the blood of a thousand students and ten thousand workers. And they're going to do it so there'll be peace. I'd like to teach junior how to ride horses and fish and cook and scuba dive and tell funny stories and why it's better in the long run to be a Victor Laszlow than a Humphrey Bogart.

Very heavy about kid telling teacher "Daddy shot by man who chased him." Let's see though. It's got a good side, it shows he's got some notion of me being hunted and he identifies. I'm not as upset as the teacher. Obviously he notices that I ain't around much and naturally it's fucking with his head. But if he can grasp the point that it was interrupted by our enemies and has nothing to do with all our feelings toward each other he'll be O.K. He might even end up a great revolutionary. I mean he's like a black kid—a Black America. The government took my daddy away. He'll have raw hate. The sort of stuff we can only intellectualize about the government. It's not so bad. The teacher's coming at this from a New York sophisticated attitude of "conflict avoidance." Generally in a separation kids just hate their fathers like crazy. So let him hate the cops and the government. He'll be O.K. He's got you and you'll teach him good from bad and how to tie his shoes and wipe his nose and I wish you were here to teach me. But well, see, I'd teach the kid like this: You got problems tying your shoes, do like Daddy did—change to boots; You got runny-nose problems—suck in the snot and spit it out in the street first chance you get.

Hey, I know this is a stupid remark, but why do your ideas of what's creative and full of self-esteem etc., sound like every other smart, Jewish, New York girl's ideas? Maybe that wasn't said just right. Let me try again. You're into too much "career" planning about your writing. You should write what moves you and give it away. You're not a professional writer. They, by the way, are a dime a dozen. The sort who end up in small print under the legend "as told to."

I'm happy in this life so *all* the past is O.K. 'cause it got me this far in one piece. I'm just in such a unique position to view life. It's just reconfirmed what I learned when I was little like junior, listening to "Row, row, row your boat . . . life is but a dream."

Dreams are for those that choose to be Dreamers and the rest is like a bottle of chicken fat getting hard in the back of my grandmother's icebox. It's reality, and a tablespoon of the stuff is essential for good chopped liver but . . . I'll take the dream that you and I and junior and all our friends old and new and all the good people in the world are gonna live lives of total ecstasy and one by one slip into Heaven where there'll be Gladys Knight records and licorice for all.

Anon E Mouse

My darling,

You've taught me how to dream. Dreams precede action. To demand the impossible first you must think it.

I've discovered this huge class of oppressed people that at the moment have no organization, no spokeswomen, no power, no money, no nothin . . . except children. Plenty of those. I'm dreaming of building a women's movement that could mobilize masses of poor women. Maybe not an impossible dream. I'm meeting other women whose heads are in similar places. But no one is making all the connections. Some are waiting, just waiting. Someone has to start.

It's scary, but then, I really have nothing to lose, have I? Now that I am responsible for myself and my child, I feel responsible for the future. Adulthood means taking responsibility for the world, acting to change it, create it. If our collective dreams don't determine the future of the planet, their corporate greed will.

Ah self-righteousness. What a high. We'll see how much lazy hedonistic me actually does. If I can just write the article to my saisfaction I'll be happy.

How come I haven't heard from you tootsie? Are you O.K.?

The more together I become, the more I lose all bitterness toward you, all desire to blame you for my own shortcomings and frustrations. Junior is away for the second week now and my activities and my fantasies are stepped up, heightened.

I should say that I may also be changing in my sexual feelings toward you, coming to a fuller appreciation of the qualities of our lovemaking. That sounds more mechanical than

I meant . . . but experience teaches. Not that I have much experience these days. Still, I don't like tepid experiences and ours were never that. Even when we quarreled and I was like an iced salmon—it was not tepid.

You're such a good man, honey. The best I've ever met.

Sorry I missed the Spanish Civil War. Wonder if it would have been as romantic a crusade if they had won. Most people think Romantics are losers. But Dostoevsky says no. "The Romantic understands everything, sees everything, more clearly than our most realistic minds see." They seek to preserve "the good and the beautiful" to the hour of their death. He is always intelligent, "the greatest rogue of all rogues. A romantic would rather go out of his mind, which rarely happens, than take open abuse. They have great faculties for contradictory sensations. They frequently become the most accomplished rascals of our time." Not a bad occupation, this romantic stuff.

I was struck with the thought that it was O.K. for me to have tried hunting but I should never do it again unless I had to eat because it was wrong to kill for fun, even if you ate what you killed and even if fun wasn't the correct word. And moreover it was doubly wrong to hunt when you yourself are being hunted. It makes you cynical besides being bad karma, because you start to visualize the world as a senseless place with everyone hunting everyone else. And that's not the way I choose to see the world even if lots of good minds see it that way. I like the way I see it and would like to continue to live and tell about my world as distinct from theirs.

What's worse than a cockroach-infested kitchen? A cockroach-infested house, naturally.

You would not believe tonight's little episode. It's about 11 P.M. and I'm alone in the apartment, peacefully deciphering Marcuse, when I go into the kitchen for a snack. All of sudden I notice maybe fifty cockroaches massed on the wall beneath the kitchen cabinet. They are perfectly still, obviously observing some special rite, such as egg laying or preparation for attack. Usually I see them one at a time (with increasing frequency ever since it got warm). I knew I might never see them grouped like that again and I should seize the time. So I climbed onto the kitchen sink very slowly and extracted the can of Hargate from the cabinet without alerting them. They seemed hypnotized. Then I took perfect aim with the aerosol and let it go, jetting them continuously before they could scatter. About a third dropped dead immediately but the rest made a run for it in every direction—at which point the can of poison ran out!

The survivors include the biggest roaches I have ever seen, so I've spent the last hour or two killing by hand the ones I could reach, but a lot have fled into the living room, and I feel so jumpy. Each time I think I've killed the last one I'm surprised by another. They're on the ceiling, the walls, the floor, the bed, the kid's room, everywhere. I can't wait until morning when I can buy another can of poison and "bomb" the entire apartment. I've tolerated their growth for too long. DEATH TO THE FASCIST INSECTS. "Armed struggle is the only path to victory."

I'm thinking if the poison doesn't work I'll buy a lizard who can live under the refrigerator and eat them. Penny swears by this method and it's also the most correct ecologically. The kid would probably love having a lizard in the house; I just wouldn't want to feel it nipping at my feet when I get up to go to the bathroom at night.

I've also heard boric acid is effective and safe, but hard to get. Hargate is supposed to be nontoxic to humans, but who knows. I'm glad the kid missed this battle with the monsters, although he, in his innocence, is not as repulsed as I am. When he sees a roach he says, "Look Mommy, a ant."

love and kisses,
the invincible A.

I must rush this. Just received and read your letters of July 12 and July 15. In a few hours I'm picking up the kid and mother at the airport, but I have to go grocery shopping first. I'm hungry. There was no food in the house while the kid was gone. I'd like breakfast but I want to do this first.

I was very moved by your description of the Indian Princess. I identified with her because I know what it's like to be a woman alone, and lonely. I know the sadness of partings from people you love, and the knowledge you may never see them again.

What worries me now about joining you is the money. The psychological problems work themselves out, but there are financial problems whether we live together or apart.

I'll write a longer letter once I am trapped home at night with the kid.

Dear man who may love another equally—

It's O.K. tootsie. We're strong, even if you insist you're only three years old. We're the same and I can't be jealous. I want you to be happy.

Junior's back. The moment I saw him again my heart flipped. He is as wonderful as I always dream he is. When he came back to the apartment with his grandma he thought you might be there. He said, "I want to see Daddy," and he cried. I said that one day we would all be together. Finally he just said, "You're my mommy," and put his arms around me.

I would definitely not link up with you permanently just for the sake of the child. Pure insanity. I mean with him being the major reason—wrong, wrong. But lately I just wonder what I have to prove to myself. I mean I've realized recently that I've already changed. I have friends, people who like me and don't know you. I enjoy being myself, my own actor upon the stage. I've already suffered and surmounted a lot of shit. So what is this with the achievement? It is rather middle-class-Jewish-girl sounding. I know what I'm capable of, but I sure chose a helluva time to prove it. Perhaps having the two weeks without the child makes me realize how impossible it is *with* him to go flying off on ideas. You were right. I was too careery for an unestablished writer. I'm on a better track now. I think I have to believe in what I'm doing to do it well. Just being apart from you I feel like I've filled in parts of myself that were missing. I can't lose them again, I don't think. The question is, do I want to live with you or without you?

I believe we can both fall in love with other people. If you were deeply in love with someone now and very serious and felt the other could slip into your life more easily and simply than I could, perhaps that is the better situation. It doesn't risk detection now, or later. It also avoids the trauma that could ruin all three of us if we didn't get along later or the circumstances were so bad we couldn't stick it out place-wise or money-wise. I know I could fall in love with the right person. But why wait around for it to happen? Why wait around for achievement? I certainly don't want a career as a free-lance writer. Organizing women I could see. But do I need that?

Right now I feel like slinking off to the woods with another human I like and cooking and playing with baby and swimming and getting stoned and watching sunsets and not thinking or at least not deciding again and again the future.

The other night was unusual. I went to this rad-chic party someplace out here in the U.S. (as differentiated from the planet known as New York City). I was pretty nervous because these are people who could recognize me if I let my guard down an instant. It's a chic, smartly dressed crowd. Good music, appetizers, grass, liquor. I keep nosing into conversation with small groups not wanting to be unsocial. I'm sort of aware I have to be somewhat nice. It sort of looks arrogant showing up with two beautiful women while some of the guys are alone and being a stranger and all, I've got to say something. The conversation gets interesting anyway, drifting from who's got the most asshole army, Turkey or Greece, to a debate about Solzhenitsyn, and most people have more info than me and are pretty enlightened. In fact I'm pretty surprised to see a few people putting him down for being a sell-out. One intellectual type says he (Solly) says, "things are better under Hitler than Stalin." Soon enough the conversation moves to women's lib as it's universally referred to in the hinterlands. I can't hold back, and ease into the discussion or rather am sucked in and venture, "Did anyone read the article on abstinence in this week's *Village Voice?*" which I thought pretty interesting. A few had and the discussion moved to a slightly higher plane. Everyone, men and women, though, were anti-women's lib, as they put it. I was really surprised. Midge Decter was referred to a lot and I really felt strange in this situation. I'm torn between not wanting to be noticed, having a certain intellectual honesty, and naturally there's always my urge to perform . . . and I blurt out, "In ten years women will be able to produce sperm and men can give birth if they have an operation." Now everyone's attention is focused on what I'm going to say, this stranger who just popped into their weekly social soirée with two of the most luscious sex objects these folks have seen in a few moons and I'm getting sort of nervous 'cause I'm sensing I'm headed for rough waters. I start to get this sharp pain . . . I think maybe my body's trying to help by giving me a heart attack. I got a real nice body. It's such a good friend. It understands all my problems. I never get mad at my body. So I excuse myself and ask for aspirins or "something stronger." The hostess gets me two Darvons and I take them for who knows what reason. The pain having long gone . . .

This afternoon I went to a cocktail party at Dotson Rader's on Central Park West. I guess it was your typical uptown literary-artsy cocktail party. I don't know because I've never been to one before. And I may not be invited to one again. A lot of writers and agents and prosperous-looking people. Interesting experience.

I met Marion Javits. I was glad to meet her because I'd been hearing intriguing things about her recently and had even read a magazine interview with her. My impression was that she was a rather liberated and outspoken woman, considering her position as a senator's wife. I thought it would be interesting to talk with her, perhaps enlist her sympathies for the plight of poor mothers. I wasn't sure exactly what I had in mind, but I figured it couldn't hurt to talk to her. Well, it was weird.

We got onto the subject of poverty and motherhood. I'm friendly, polite and warm because I'm confident this is a safe topic of mutual agreement (after all, I'm not going to sing the praises of Ramsey Clark, her husband's opponent in the Senate race, that would not be tactful). I mean, who cannot sympathize with struggling motherhood? What mother cannot lament the poverty of her less fortunate sisters.

Well, right away the reaction is uptightness and disagreement. "You use such old-fashioned words." She sneers. "You mean desperate, not destitute. Desperate because of their emotional state, their anxieties and worries." I can't believe what I'm hearing. Is she really offering me this doublethink? I answer, "Sure I'm talking about desperate women. They feel desperate because they are destitute. Have you been to East New York recently?" She shakes her head wearily. "Women in this coun-

86

try are not destitute. In other parts of the world they are."

I ask her if she's been to Arab countries where women wear the veil. She says she's been to Iran and remarks that polygamy creates an interesting sexual situation for the women. Something about how since the women only get fucked on a rotating basis they try to make the most of it when their turn comes up (of course she didn't say "fuck"). She says she's talked to women who dig this setup and she gets into a defense of the Eastern customs. "Some people choose to fence themselves in. Don't knock it 'til you've tried it."

"Choose! Those women don't have any choice," I reply. I'm wondering if she is secretly, slyly, "putting me on." If I cannot get her to condemn concubinage I shall assume I am home in bed dreaming this conversation.

With each sentence the conversation becomes more surreal. I had expected polite, gracious chitchat. I am not a debater or into confrontation, but I find myself forced to respond to what she is saying. I become more and more aggressive as she, too, warms to the subject. She says poverty is a personal problem. The individual must work his way up. Look at the Jews, look at the Irish, look at her and Jake.

Behind all the arguments I offer her I sense the blankness of my own astonishment. My role surprises me. Here I am, in an elegant room, defending the poor and the powerless. Today I am even dressed like the others; no one could spot me. And the ideas I'm laying out are not even outrageous. They are your basic liberal-feminist axioms.

She tells me impatiently that Jake votes for daycare and guaranteed income. He is not against these things but she is obliged to differ with me philosophically. "There will always be the poor," she says.

I am so fascinated I cannot let her go. In a spirit of polite reconciliation we get into a personal discussion of child rearing. She says her proudest accomplishments were raising her children. Of course we differ on child-rearing methods as well. There is no doubt that she is stricter and more into rules. The generation gap yawns between us. Then comes the crunch.

"Where's Abbie?" she asks.

"I don't know, but if I did I wouldn't say."

"Abbie must be a difficult person," she says. "Isn't he really a bit out of his mind?"

I am amazed at this sideswipe and stare at her, speechless.

"Yes, I'm sure he is," she says. "I can tell by the expression on your face."

So that's the reason for the uptightness and the negative attitude. Marion Javits will not let herself agree about anything with the wife of A - - - - H - - - - - -. Mind you, I have not mentioned her husband at all, and he's an easy target these days with the scandal about his campaign contributions from big corporations. I did not approach her with the idea of initiating a predictable clichéd argument based on our husbands' politics. And even as she expanded her attack on you and everything you stand for, I refrained from bringing in Jake. I just refused to sink to that level. I defended you, of course, and our ideals, but she refused to understand what I was talking about. I guess it's not chic to be radical anymore.

My feminism had whispered "build bridges," but you can't build bridges over an ocean. I won't easily forget the icy cynicism beneath the sophisticated liberal style. Her words still echo in my head, "desperate, not destitute. It's a state of mind."

Yipppeeeeeeee! We all belong on the psychoanalyst's couch, us poor mothers. Maybe I should tell Lydia, a Puerto Rican mother I met, to go for therapy. She could explore the implications of why she's always hungry after meals. She's the one who stopped drinking milk in order to have enough for her son. Or maybe Virginia could benefit from some Freudian analysis. Her problem is that her daughter stopped attending school because she was ashamed of her rags. Maybe I'll start a therapy group. We could begin with consciousness raising, move on to psychodrama at the welfare centers, and complete our "cure" with "encounter sessions" at H.E.W.

Dotson was charming and kind as ever, and expressed his concern for you. I think he would enjoy meeting the kid, next time.

The monkey was still awake when I got home so we played until I put him to bed. Now I must go back to work on the article.

Hope you're having as much fun as I am!

What a strange love, smuggled across enemy lines.

I want to respond to all your terrific thoughts about poor women. You are exactly on track. You have hit the vital nerve of the women's movement head on and helped expand it. Don't get too high on the horse, even though your position is correct. Struggle can function on a multitude of levels. Thus it's not "bad" that intellectual white women contemplate the question of who should be on top when balling while black women worry about where the fuck they're going to find a bed to do it in in the first place. You get the point, even if badly stated.

If you become an organizer of welfare mothers I'd be overpowered with such pride. I've seen great poverty in my travels among blacks and Indians and chicanos in cities and country. I've spent a good deal of time with the poor because I know they'd never recognize me and I can be a little looser knowing I'm safe in that respect.

I feel lucky. Not lucky to be alive but lucky to be alive and me. A whacked-out, lonely fugitive wandering the highways of wrongs to be righted, battles won, experience tasted and dreams to be dreamed and still not knowing how to read a compass. Lucky me.

When I was little I used to fight all the school bullies and after finally being overpowered, back bloody raw against the pebbled schoolyard, the battle would end. The bully would win a hollow victory. For there was no force on earth to make me say the magic word "uncle," which in our neighborhood meant surrender. And all the other kids would pick me up and slap me on the back and brush my cuts and say, "He was bigger but you put up a hell of a fight. You're the best scrapper in the school." No bully ever fought me twice. Winning was worse than losing. Such a clever little fucker to realize you can never lose by fighting bigger kids. How come people have trouble learning that? Tell me some day. It's so easy. I think that's the great feeling that overwhelms me on the eve of the recommendation for the impeachment of the President of the United States. Only the Bullies have the capacity to be humiliated.

Right now I'm having a lambchop marathon with the kid. I have to sit here at this fucking table with him for five minutes for each tiny grain of meat that goes in. Meat which I deny myself but he wastes. Of course I ended up eating it—but without any pleasure since by then it was cold.

I'm pretty jumpy these days. We have heard that the two arresting cops visited my mother's apartment building and spoke to the super in May '73—four months before the bust. The super let them both into my mother's apartment too. Can you imagine! More is coming out on this and I will keep you informed. The case looks very exciting. My poor mother, to be dragged in again and again, and used this way. I've just learned that the FBI has obtained her phone records from the telephone company in their continuing search for you. Why can't she be allowed to live her life in peace. Hasn't the FBI heard of the generation gap? I'm also worried that when my article is published it will bring increased attention from the IRS, the FBI and Welfare.

Saw *State of Siege* the other night. Quite good. I'm sure they filmed it in Allende's Chile before the coup 'cause I was in Santiago years and years before and I recognized it. How ironic. I read somewhere that the U.S. exports 95 percent of the world's torture machines.

I had such a vivid dream last night. You and I were together in the Future. Everything was super-modern and computerized. We were at a fancy apartment-hotel with shops and restaurants in the lobby. The staff was all women. Women like the cop's wives I worked with when I was a Pinkerton summer cop: young and attractive in a plastic way, but tough and dumb. Their job was to make sure everyone followed the rules.

Women could get free manicures on seats that swiveled around the ceiling of the high, big lobby. Suddenly I was up in the air getting a manicure, and I didn't want one, but I almost fell through space trying to get out of the traveling automated chair. Even though the apartments were luxurious, people were crowded into them and privacy was scarce. At least that's how the female cops lived, because I wandered into one of their rooms by mistake.

Anyway I guess I didn't like the future 'cause I was trying to get out of the building. I was alone at this point. I ran down flights of stairs trying to escape and ended up on the second-level basement, but something scared me and I left quickly. I ran up many flights of stairs, then realized I'd left my shoes down there. A matron in the lobby said I could get them back by filing a note with the computer.

Suddenly you were there, helping me. Your features were tiny and your skin wrinkled, as though successive operations had made your face shrivel. I felt sad about your face. You weren't bad looking, just different. And I loved you. But we had to fill out the computer form perfectly in computerese language in order to get my shoes back, otherwise the computer would reject the card. After it was all filled out I realized I

93

had to put my name on the card, but there was no space for names. You said it wasn't necessary, but I was sure it was. We argued a little in a friendly way and I started to put my name on the back of the card. Then I woke up.

I see the Sphinx and it is a very delicious part of my life. I don't know how to sort this all out emotionally though I have confidence everyone's moving forward with honesty and good faith. There is no doubt she's brought super-happiness to my life. I don't see how I can put any of this into context until we actually meet and get to know each other. We might have changed more than we suspect. I'm not upset and don't feel trapped or pushed to make decisions on this score. You should, however, know of her existence and that it's more than a casual relationship, and you should feel free to pursue your desires, not only carnal but emotional. She's no lightweight and teaches me a lot about survival. She is better at this than me, as you are. I think there's some truth to women keeping secrets better than men. I think I sense why. It has to do with channeled upbringing about passive-aggressive differences. Women have fewer people to talk to, thus fewer to tell anything, never mind just secrets. If I added up the thirty or so people I've come closest to in my life I'd have to say very few, less than five, would be male. I think I only had one period of "hanging out with the boys" in my life—at one point during my first unhappy marriage and then only for six months. I think "hanging out with the boys" is very common among males.

I get sad sometimes. Very sad. I think we'd get along very nicely. Do you think we made a mistake having a child? I never asked that or felt it ever before. Somehow it all doesn't seem quite fair to him. He doesn't get to make a lot of choices. Give him a hug and kiss for me. I can't write more.

Dear City,

It's almost a year since the bust. It's good to hear all the new dirt the investigators are digging up. I wish I had been able to talk about the case more, publicly, before I went under. But the lawyers kept advising against it in view of the other defendants. I would have discussed it long ago if it hadn't been for that. Remember that speech at Harvard Law School? I was a real student of the judicial system, but I was absolutely sure I couldn't get a fair trial even though I had no previous drug busts. Gerry [Lefcourt] and I have been going to trial for six years. He said in the end it would be my word against the cops and unless our defense could discredit the cops I'd lose, 'cause sure as hell they could discredit me. The D.A. would introduce books and speeches I had made saying dope was O.K., telling people how to buy and sell it.

You should also put into the computer the numerous death threats I received late nights from supposed Zippies or other assorted nuts. Your mamma also got'em, and it was always a mystery how or why anyone would go to such trouble to track me down and get the number. That always bothered me. So few people knew I was staying there and almost no one knew where it was or your mother's name. It was unlisted, then, anyway, which adds fuel to the suspicion that cops were watching. It's too bad we can't sit down and sort this out face to face.

After reading your letters I had to really do some soul searching about what if someone yells "ally-ally-in-free" and I can reappear. I'm fairly certain I would announce myself.

My darling—

I've decided to go through with organizing as much as I can. By the way, just got hold of a copy of *Prairie Fire*. Do you know of it? The book published privately by the Weather Underground. It's hard to get a copy, although it's public. The book describes "the politics of revolutionary anti-imperialism." It analyzes the forces operating in the world now and in the past, and indicates, in a general way, what needs to be done. They don't lay out any blueprints but that's what makes the book so stimulating. I can see my own practical ideas fitting into their ideological framework. The language is a little stiff, so I don't see the book as a popular document so much as an organizer's handbook. It is clear and direct, however, and the book gets more profound the more times I read it.

What has happened? I haven't heard from you for the longest time? I'm lost and can't find you. Are you at the Bolshoi ballet? Picketing the Bolshoi ballet? At home in bed? At Max's? Has Max's gone bankrupt like I read in the paper? We're getting old, like the other generation weeping when they closed Lindy's or the Brass Rail and the Roxy Theater got cut up into eighty Orange Juliuses. Well, Max's was ours—lousy food (except for the shrimp cocktail) and all. Say high to Mickey and tell him I'll drop by some day. About four months ago (don't remember if I told you) I had a dream that my gang and I entered New York City and they went into Max's with machine guns and told everyone "be calm and no one is gonna get hurt" and they ripped out the phones and then I came in out of a car with blacked windows. Went through the door straight to the table I liked best and ordered a double shrimp cocktail and a pitcher of sangria. Ate chick peas waiting (they have a terrific taste—but nostalgia for me now) and told Mickey to play it cool. It'd help business and if the service was fast I'd be out in a coupla minutes. He was glad to see me and said he'd put it on my bill. It was a nice dream, done in thirties costumes.

I heard a strange rumor that you were sure I would end up living with someone and forget all about you. That you actually said this to someone. I didn't think it was true. Just telling you so you get some idea about how rumors fly and get distorted and filtered. The question "What's happening?" has always made me giggle but now it takes on cosmic, comic dimensions. Can I play Jean Dixon and make a few predictions? Country rock will grow bigger. The Prophet replaces Jesus Christ. Ted

Kennedy will make it exactly like fourteen years ago when his brother won. There will be a rush of enthusiasm for changing the world. Huge wave of liberal legislation. Nationalize many things. Railroads first. Government agency cracking down on multinational corporations. It won't be the same as the other Kennedy period. Too many lost dreams under the pillow groaning at night. It's all there in Joan Kennedy's face (she's greeting Lenny Bernstein at Tanglewood after her "recuperation"), the picture is worth a thousand columns. Revolution breaks out in Argentina, and Brazil moves troops and tanks in. The Weather Underground will come alive with a rash of bombings of U.S. corporations. Amnesty will be granted to Vietnam deserters just before Saigon falls. Most won't come back but those that do will get big media attention so it will look like "everyone's glad to get back to the good old U.S.A." Ford will do it as a big gesture-of-unity theme. It's a natural. The stereo is yelling Ro Coodah, or however you spell his name. I'm stuffing chicken for dinner. How did I ever end up in the kitchen anyway, basting chickens. I love it. . . . Pot pills are a natural cure for skinny people. Where are the hotshit scientists? Marco Polo did not go to China for spaghetti, he went for dope, all the explorers were heads. History has lied about dope all along. America's made two contributions to the dope world. Tobacco and corn whiskey—not much. Miss a stoned session with you. I miss your letters and communications. Miss answers to questions. Does Ramsey Clark have a chance? He and I had some good talks. Are you in trouble? I worry. I'm fine.

your jungle buddy, Tarzan

Very exciting news in the case. The lawyers have an affidavit from my mother's building superintendent which says that in May both arresting cops visited him and one was in uniform. My mother, you will recall, was still in Florida then. The super let them into my mother's apartment and they stayed there a half-hour. When they entered, one of them went into her bedroom, shut the door and stayed there five minutes. I'm sure he bugged the phone in there. The super also gave them a duplicate key to the apartment for future visits! More and more is coming out. There was definitely surveillance of you in May, June and July preceding the bust. The investigation is proceeding as fast as it can. We will move for hearings to prove wiretapping occurred. Since the cops have denied this, we could get the case thrown out. There is a problem of timing, however. We need time to nail down all our leads but the judge is impatient to dispose of the cases of the other defendants. If the hearing occurs too soon our sources of information will dry up.

I find myself wondering if my place is big enough for three! Oh, I better hold that dream until we can *prove* everything. Our investigator is going to be the hero of this case. He's determined to break it and has been working on his own time lately. He's real nice.

There seems to be a snafu with the mail.

I also had a bit of shit fit reading the long exposé of the Brotherhood which was surprisingly long in coming. I expect a book on it. The *Voice* piece was actually fairly superficial and the writer relied on trial transcripts for the bulk of the info, from what I know. Naturally what upset me the most was the last paragraph about Leary talking to the FBI. When folks are squeezed, especially ones who have something to lose, they can talk. Billy Hitchcock is the world's lowest sonofabitch. All Leary is accused of is being a salesman for Orange Sunshine, and Leary's concern was that kids didn't burn out. They also kept the price down way low (two bucks or under) so I can't really see equating them with the Mafia. That's ridiculous. Leary, I'm fairly certain, didn't reap any profits. The author makes a strong hint on that score, wondering where he got his money, forgetting his popularity on the campus lecture circuit and his books. Besides, Leary wouldn't be in jail in the first place if it hadn't been for his notoriety, not for any act he or his daughter may have performed. But the *Village Voice* has always been antidope (half the writers are found scraping themselves off the floor of the Lion's Head each night). Hitchcock could have skipped when they squeezed him. He has international hideouts and sanctuaries, instead he turned on his closest friend.

Leary's information must be pretty stale by now, but it is an awful blow to people's morale. If true, it confirms what revolutionary critics of dope have been saying for some time. Granted we never saw Leary as a revolutionary. Not even when he was parroting slogans. He did, however, make a contribution to the cutting loose of a generation from the cultural morass which feeds the cancer of capitalism and imperialism. His personality faults were known to us all, but his ass was on the line. I liked him a lot as you know, and am saddened and troubled to hear he's talking to federal authorities. That seemed to me the only "crime" he's committed, if true. The Brotherhood was a nationalist group in terms of the counterculture. It's not revolutionary any more than say a feminist magazine or a black owned and controlled bank. Not by itself, but any revolutionary force has to come to terms with nationalist institutions, be they internal or external (i.e., Algeria, Mexico, Egypt, Ghana and practically most of the Third World countries fighting imperialism). In the U.S. in the absence of proletariat struggle to any significant degree, in the absence of an organized communist party, the only serious hope for change and mobilization against the forces of authority are cultural: race, sex, age, lifestyle, unless, of course, you want to jump on the reformist bandwagon and swallow the lie that people like Ralph Nader, Sam Erwin and Carole King are going to make the world revolution and create a socialist America.

Nationalism has always been the puzzle box of revolution. It's right on and right off simultaneously, but in no way is it the enemy. It's a force with mass appeal that must be reckoned with.

Michael Boyd Randall, currently a fugitive, was and is in no way a bad egg. He was a champion rebel and I wish him well and also his comrades on the lam and those that got sacrificed in the cages of California prisons because a few mamma's rich boys got squeamish when threatened by the feds. If they had held tight they could have all been free today. You met some of them in the old days. Leary is as guilty of ripping off bread as Sigmund Freud can be accused of founding psychoanalysis for the money. I can't accept that. Every check ol' Timmy gave us bounced. If he talks though, he's committing the one crime abhorrent to all outsiders: direct collaboration with the enemy. He is committing others to the cages he has grown to loathe. Perhaps if he had entered prison detesting the institution rather than floating off into his cloudy, mystical nonsense this wouldn't have happened. I hope all our friends are safe.

I should say something about drugs because they are an easy scapegoat for leftist theoreticians. They are a cultural divider and hence important. I maintain there's a narcotics-law problem, not a drug problem in the ghettos, that the greatest tragedy of the "drug problem" is the fact that cops send people to prison, break up homes, gangs, all sorts of indigenous units and use drugs as a pretext to invade the black community. White institutional drugs are allowed, and black "street drugs" are used as an excuse to terrorize the community. Drugs probably wouldn't be any more important than countercultural music, except for the fact that the institutions in power have gone to war.

Drugs have no intrinsic value. All communist countries have correctly outlawed them. There are loads of other exhilarating ways to get high. Communist governments have a cultural revolution to achieve that is national in scope. Our task in the U.S. is to build countercultural institutions that make the raising of children breeding grounds for revolution and rebellion against the wishes of the dominant, decadent culture. If we've learned anything over the past few years it's that politics and cultural struggle are blurred. I think any observer, say, of the disruption and revolt in the army must conclude that the basis of soldiers' alienation from the military system was cultural, and class was a secondary phenomenon. It's no great wonder to me that America's great contribution to the world will be cultural. It's no wonder there is no active leftist party in the U.S. as there is in every European country.

It's very hard to write with so many questions unanswered.

I'm at a total loss. I've just read my very first long letter to you (I kept a copy) and it's a thousand moons ago. I feel very far from you in many ways. Every effort people pledged to make seems to have been forgotten. Meanwhile I've been moving steadily down another road. This fall looms ahead like fog-shrouded woods. I don't feel lonely or alone. I'm neither. I just feel adrift. Adrift from all that. Sparks of hope. Rays of energy. But on the whole new times, new concerns are engulfing us all.

I missed seeing your piece in the *Voice*. It was some shock to pick it up eagerly hoping to see stuff by you and discover this whole Leary mess instead.

"So round and round and round and round we go. . . ."

Well, I did it. I hope I have started my own little contribution to the world-wide trouble-making conspiracy. I brought together fifteen welfare mothers—all young, interesting and happy to be there. We're going to try to become a group. Next week there'll be more talk, planning, communion, god knows what else. I'm not pushing for action until we all have a good idea what the right one is. I want group cohesion to form so we're together when we need to act. The right action, though, is important to encourage people to stay with it, to involve them, and to spread the word. I am by no means the leader. Everyone is articulate and has ideas. It will be interesting to see how collective we become and/or who emerges as leaders. All of it will emerge. We want to go slow, but everyone senses the needs. Yowie. Zowie! I'm excited. It was such a good starting mixture. If it stays alive we can branch out.

The main problems I see are, (1) developing a wide base, (2) deciding when the right time is for the first action and what it should be, (3) designing demonstrations and media trips without risking unnecessary arrests and/or violence to women and children who might really be wiped out by extra hassles. Actually most of the women in the room seemed not turned off to militant struggle. All agreed that you can go far in that direction if you have a large enough number of people. Safety in groups. The day that me and kiddo are busted along with lots of mommies and kids will be a proud one. Although I'd rather win demands than be busted. If there's a depression coming there are going to be a lot of dissatisfied people. Got to get ready. All of us.

We're going to meet once a week, at suppertime, with the

kiddies, who will go to another apartment with a volunteer babysitter. We're trying to get some welfare experts to come talk to us—radical social workers, lawyers and organizers from the old National Welfare Rights Organization.

God, I'm so high. Adrenalin pumping with all the possibilities glittering before me. If we can only pull it off. Push, push, and make it happen.

I'm shy and nervous about leadership. What is it? I want to make things happen, yet . . . sometimes I bend over backwards out of a sense of modesty. I'm so tired of feeling sad and helpless. I want to change the world again. When you feel you're working for change you don't get so depressed about evil in the world. It scares you less because you're grappling with it; you see your opponent up close from an engaged position. When I sit here and think of what they have done to us and what they are doing to the world, I just know I don't want to be a victim anymore. I think of the Jara family and realize how lucky we are. We still have time to act. I used to feel guilty about Them, the poor. Now that I am one of them I've begun to realize my only hope is anger.

All I've done so far is start something. Now I'm trying to assess what I need to do, to learn. The hardest part, the sustained struggle, is still ahead. Teach me everything you've got, baby, and we'll fly off to heaven with Batboy!

It's right. It's right, what I'm doing. And I discovered it all by myself. The more I grow, the more I do, the better I become, the closer I feel to you. Sometimes I think I understand you in totally new ways. The ecstasy of writing well, or playing out an idea and making it real, these are new for me, but you've always known them.

I'll write more later. Just wanted to share my excitement with you. I feel like a baby who's taken her first step.

Love,
me

Depressing news two days ago. The stock market's gone down 102 points in three weeks. The depression is starting. I'm worried. Everyone will be poor, like us.

I have a lot of ideas and scenarios in my head for depression days. How far can the welfare system extend itself? Perhaps those on welfare will be the lucky few. I think the time is approaching for Robin Hood behavior on the part of revolutionary groups. Redistribution of food at the point of a gun. Stealing food and giving it to the poor. There will be a lot of grocery holdups anyway, so the object is to make them political acts to everyone concerned. I think the Tupamaros have done things like that. The point is, I know I myself have fantasies of doing that, if forced to, so why not in a revolutionary context? I feel strongly the radical left must prepare for the depression, which, coming after Watergate, will create hordes of desperate, disillusioned people.

I love you and miss you. This separation is making me appreciate you all over again. I feel that when we reunite I will gaze into your eyes and all the same old love will overwhelm me and I'll cry. I've become self-conscious about writing to you, inhibited. Feel there is nothing much to say. Anything new that happens, I write, but the rest is interior goings on, sometimes boredom, sometimes excitement, sometimes fear of the future. But I am definitely past nostalgia. You hit it right on the mark. I, too, cannot look back because the present and the future are too exciting. I've passed the point of no return and feel very committed to the future, to my continued, varied life. Somehow in the last two months with all the boredom of the hot city summer I passed a turning point. I think it was writing something I was proud of and organizing the meeting, simple as that sounds. Inside, I feel different about myself.

Dear Babes,

Well, things have certainly gone complicated routes, *n'est-ce pas?* It's been almost two months since I heard from you. Communication is totally kaputo. I can't even remember questions I've asked you. I'm not even sure I could pick you out in a crowd. In point of fact I sense we are totally apart. If that's our own choosing or the work of the gods that toss down obstacles in our path, I haven't yet been able to fathom.

Also, of course, I'm digesting news of Herr Doktor Leary, the swine. It's obvious to me he's talked his fucking demented head off to the Gestapo. Especially that bastard D.A. Thompson in Chicago who was the last prick to try me in court. God, Leary is disgusting. It's not just a question of being a squealer but a question of squealing on people who *helped* you. I'm really upset. I've never even had cause to use the word opportunist before, it's laced with so many meanings, but Leary fits the bill perfectly. I'm stunned. Can you imagine turning state's evidence on people who allegedly helped you? The curses crowd my mouth. Nothing has ever happened like this that I can think of, can you? It's not like the Communists who testified against their comrades in the fifties. It's not like Phillip Abbott Luce who gave testimony against people he went to Cuba with. It's not even like one bank robber who gets caught snitching out the others. This is incredible. Timothy Leary is a name worse than Benedict Arnold. It's not just a matter of changing sides. The Dos Passos 180-degree twist for example when he went from Commie to cop faster than a silver buck. I can't imagine anything close except children turning parents in under Nazi Germany. Stalin once turned in his own chief spy in China just to earn Mao's confidence. What a rat.

I'm not down though. Everything is going incredible. I'm totally content in my new life. I'm not bouncing like a cork. I'm digging in to this identity. And everything is peaking. I'm hunching the delay out on lover's limb and suspecting you're most likely going your way. If true that's O.K.—did you hear that??? I mean it. I'm prepared to sever relations because two months and no word is like a one-way dialogue. November meeting is OUT. No meeting possible until December and possibly not 'til Christmas which also has problems. I can't get into the whys but this different-life business is complicated and much advance planning is needed. I told you how I have this incredibly complex calendar. There are travel necessities. This pales to my new life responsibilities. This pales to the recognition safety factor. I was more or less recognized about two weeks ago. A look-alike situation I got through, but you're never sure and it grinds into your gut when it happens.

Maybe it's the lousy mails. If we were playing chess by mail I would have eaten all the pieces by now, licking imaginary stamps for dessert.

Your pen pal hanging in there but dancing to other drummers.

Emilia Hearhard.

I'm reading a good book, a paperback called *Woman as Revolutionary*. It describes many women I hadn't known about, with excerpts from their speeches and writings. One of my favorites is Olympe de Gouges. She and the proletarian women in France founded the club of the knitters, the Tricotreuses, during the French Revolution. They dared to attack the leading male revolutionaries, who, the book says, were the greatest foes of the emancipation of women. Olympe wrote that "marriage is the grave of trust and love," and she proclaimed the right of women to have children without paternity. After the revolution, sure enough, women were prohibited from taking part in the political life, and Olympe was guillotined after attacking Robespierre for the excesses of the Terror and the execution of Louis XVI. I wonder why she objected to the execution of the king—was it a reversion to her class origins or was it more complicated than that, involving her quarrels with Robespierre and the males of the revolutionary tribunal responsible for the Terror?

Now I'm getting chills reading a speech by "La Pasionaria," Dolores Ibarruri. Incredible eloquence: "Fascism shall not pass because the wall of bodies with which we have barred its way today is strengthened by weapons of defense we have captured from the enemy—a cowardly enemy because he has not the ideas which lead us into battle. The enemy therefore has no dash and impetuosity whereas we are borne on the wings of our ideas, of our love, not for the Spain which is dying together with the enemy, but for the Spain we want to have— a democratic Spain."

I feel awful that you haven't heard from me. I've sent you at least nine letters in the past two months. Though you sound more than usually alienated from me (a perfect right to after two months without mail), I am not from you. No matter what happens between us or doesn't, I want to help you.

There was another installment in the *Voice* about Leary last week, and a press conference was held in San Francisco at which even his son denounced him. I heard a tape of it on the radio. It was powerful. I heard also that Leary was up for parole in a year and probably would have gotten out, but that he is flipped out and felt he was losing public attention.

Huey Newton jumped bail a few weeks ago and has gone underground.

I'm hoping to raise some money for the defense committee this week so we'll have enough to continue the investigation.

Last week is sort of like a blank: I worked like crazy trying to write a short story, but I felt guilty about spending time on fictional pursuits. I ran into trouble with one scene, no matter how I wrote it I couldn't get it right. Instead of giving up I bulldozed my way through until I finished a reasonable edition two days ago. Now it's nighttime and I'm afraid to look the piece over. Afraid I'll hate most of it. Yet the idea is good and worth doing well, if I can. Part of my problem, I suspect, is that since it's fiction I'm reminded of my earlier masterpiece and then I lose all confidence. If it's not good enough as a story I'll send it to you as a letter. It's a pretty accurate description of one afternoon in which nothing happened.

I've hardly spoken to a soul all week, except for the kid. In these writing spells I lose sight of everything including my body; nothing exists for me. I race through everything to get back to work. It's a good life, actually, and I wish it could continue indefinitely. Getting stoned and dancing has been my most reliable joy giver lately. Sometimes I invite people over but I feel my place isn't that pleasant to sit in, unless you're totally devoted to me.

Dear one,

My article is coming out in this week's *Voice,* finally. Hope you like it. I'm such a novice that I'm excited!

Am becoming a little active politically through my local church. I've gone to a study group and assorted meetings of the left. They puzzle me. They seem unable to respond to anything unless they read it or it's a hand-me-down idea. Anyway I'm trying to find out what's going on. Although the city seems outwardly peaceful and rather dead, there are a surprising number of meetings going on, with many people active.

I'm having fun.

I cannot afford sitters anymore, so I sit here, in my usual spot in the bedroom–living room. Sometimes I work and sometimes I just think, why should I work if I get no rewards? The piece has not been published in the *Voice* yet, and I don't know when it will be or if it will be, anymore. I don't know how I'll meet the rent, much less the phone bill this month (I have this fantasy the FBI will step in and offer to pay it), and I'm lonely. There is no one to share problems with, or ideas. There is no relief. There is no logic in nature which guarantees fairness. How did I get to the bottom of this well? All my problems are real but they are so heavy I'm beginning to wonder if there's something wrong with me, and not the world.

I saw Roberta a few days ago. She said to me, "Why not do things from a position of strength instead of weakness and crisis? Why not take care of your own security first and then tackle the other problems?" Then she said, "Why are you organizing? Why not work as a psychologist or a social worker?"

And I said, "Because I'm alienated, that's why. Because I want to write and I want to tear it down." And I felt flooded with bitterness and was surprised by the intensity of my reaction to her friendly advice.

I went home thinking about what she said. I've always had a lot of respect for her, so I had to think about it. Her advice is the same advice I got six months ago from Natalie, from Barbara, from my mother and from my sister. "Feather your own nest first," they say, "then act from strength." I understand the point about acting from strength but I think when you get busy with the nest you never act, period. You always want more and you become greedy. My worries about eviction and bills are a drag and sometimes they immobilize me. By god, nothing's been going good lately. Maybe I am crazy, but I do not want to give in. I will not sell the time of my life.

Roberta couldn't understand my yen for the pizza man down the street, either. She said it sounded "risky."

Are you in love (deeply) with someone else? Honesty is the best policy between us. I know you still love me so I really wouldn't be hurt or feel more lonely if it were so.

The investigation sounds incredible. To try and answer all your questions. There is nothing inconsistent with my whereabouts or behavior that contradicts any of the investigator's findings. I'm astonished they seemed to have used classic N.Y.P.D. squad tactics of tapping described in my last book.

In that period I was the spearhead of a lawsuit against the Intelligence Division of the N.Y.P.D. True, there were other groups listed as plaintiffs but most of those groups vanished. You know the lifespan of a movement group is about a year. The suit took a couple. I think I was the only individual listed. Certainly the most prominent, and the press played it up as my suit. I remember seeing all this on page one of the *Times* story. Now I know the mentality of the Red Squad guys and I think the lawyer does. They had to destroy a million files because of that suit and eat a lot of public shit. If it had happened six months later, after Watergate was real big, they would have looked much worse and everyone would have raised a bigger stink about it. Imagine the Police Commissioner of New York City in a press conference admitting that the Red Squad had a file on one out of eight citizens in New York. I find that unbelievable. To think there was no outcry or demand for independent investigation by civilian groups is peculiar, don't you think?

Anyways they must have been pissed at me and I don't mean generally pissed. I mean *specifically* pissed. So a cousin of a cop spots me. That's easy. Everyone in the building got a charge out of knowing I was staying there. The staff called me by name. O.K., he tells his cousin, "Guess who lives where I work?" and this comes right after the P.D. is fuming about this exposé of their intelligence system forced on them by that fucking hippie bastard. They decide to do a little snooping— maybe free-lance it. They find out about the book I'm working on* and everything else falls into place. I think I even interviewed a dope dealer there but he insisted on blasting the radio and talking only in the kitchen. Here I was gathering info on dope peddling and they got me under surveillance.

---

* *Book of the Month Club Selection,* a survival manual written by Abbie in 1973 as a partial sequel to *Steal This Book*. No one will publish it, even though *Steal This Book* was a best seller.

Today they finally published my article, but I feel so beaten down from the uncertainties of the past few weeks that I cannot rise to the occasion.

The awful title they gave it didn't surprise me. I knew they would stress the wife angle since that's the only way they know me. But they took out more at the last minute than I had expected. Some good lines went, and most of the political analysis at the end. At this point, I'm just happy to see it in print. People are saying nice things to me about it, so I am getting a reward. I won't complain. I guess these days you always end up paying a little more than you expected.

The investigator thinks those Zippie phone calls were actually the cops checking to see if you were in.

High one,

Got the *Voice* today. My hand trembled when I grabbed a copy and folded it quickly under my arm. I would have to be a cold-blooded fugitive indeed to have been able to approach that corner with total casualness. I bought a few other mags for camouflage, paid with lowered head and left the newsstand. It was in town. Town can be awkward for me at first. I have haunting fears of being recognized, of being snatched off the street suddenly. I dreamed I saw the kid last night. I was sad when I awoke. Angel understands everything. She's always a comfort. She's made a potential nightmare into a paradise. She's not jealous of my feelings for you. I have no idea how this all works out in the future but somehow it doesn't plague me since so much of the future is out of my hands.

Coming into the city is dangerous as is changing spots. Who knows what's real. It just seems dangerous. My eyes dart behind dark glasses quickly taking in everyone's presence. It's a good development—casing a joint before you enter, I mean. So I was in a danger zone and the *Voice* popped up and our names sticking out, I grabbed the issue and ran. I walked six blocks to a park and sat down and read the piece. It was very exciting. Let's see. I didn't like them capitalizing on my name and I had the feeling they chopped some off your account of welfare mothers. It bounced a few times. You had some very good lines. The lioness was an excellent allusion and in general your threads for holding different elements together very good. You have an I-dragged-myself-to-the-typewriter attitude, your idea about work, ambition, etc., which I think is good because most readers can identify with that. I don't like sentences such as, "Perhaps it is the role of woman. . . ." It either is or *is not*. There's no room for "perhaps" when you want to change things. I think I agree with the *Voice* people who said it was two articles because each section doesn't get developed enough. But there are lots of good ideas and you have an interesting vantage point. You leave yourself open for "chops" though. Complaining about poverty with references to "the color TV set" and "the $7,600 the IRS says we owe them" without adding the fact that we gave all that bread away. A long time ago I told you you had a tendency to actually underplay harassment and adversity. It's not a question of lying or distorting reality. It's a question of focusing your pen as if it were a spotlight and showing the reader what you choose to show. The harassment by the FBI should be banged down the throat of *Voice* readers. It all reads too casually, that part. The *Voice* has a style reflected typically in the piece on Plimpton and Goldstein's coverage of Fellini's party. Every issue has to have at least two pieces like this. A reporter drags him/herself to a party bemoaning the fact that the same old faces are there and tries to do a Tom Wolfe dissection of the event without the talent or space for such. Both parties covered in the same old *Voice* treatment. I've been at a few of those parties and the only "same old face" was the *Village Voice* reporter's and Fred McDarrah telling everyone they no longer had celebrity status as he busily snapped rolls of pictures of them.

I have a good book proposal—too flippant for you, but timely and catchy. You can pass it on to friends. A book about the really "Good Old Days . . ." or how the Romans amused themselves waiting for the empire to collapse. It's a research book not written for its historical content but with an eye to today's decadence buffs. Chapters describing the Circuses.

They got incredibly elaborate near the end—wilder than any Alice Cooper or David Bowie concert. There were sets in the Coliseum where mock wars were staged, with mountains, rivers and temples erected, hundreds slaughtered in costume, wild animals of every description forced into combat and then everything climaxing in the grand bonfire. Then there could be a section on drinks and one on food, with recipes, etc. Then a section on sexual practices with a how to do a true-to-life Roman orgy in your basement for $27.50 and a coupla pounds of grapes. Then a section on travel—how and where the Roman tourists did it, and a section on sports. Maybe dope. . . . Like it?

Back to your piece. I liked it, wanted to read more and felt cut off—thus I suggested two pieces but you probably wanted to see something in print and now it's there, so let's get on with it

I'm reading *Prairie Fire* and may get a review off, I'll see. I like the book. It's very stimulating to know there's some group out there acting and also taking the time and energy to reflect on *why* they are acting and need to act more. I'm a big fan of the Weatherpeople. I can't find any real disagreement with their ideas, their actions, their structure or whatever. They are a true revolutionary group, absolutely the most international of all revolutionary groups with the possible exception of the Japanese group operating out of Holland. They have a woman head, I forget their name.

Reading of the kid was both exciting and sad. The kid dancing in my dream last night was very vivid. I've been staring at his photo lost in thought. Thoughts go from there to the dedication page of *Prairie Fire* and all those prisoners' names—really sad, people have to remember them. I felt very indebted to you, champion of my freedom. Felt luckier than the people on the list. Think how many go off to jail totally innocent but without enough mon for investigations so they have to cop pleas. I'm glad I took off . . . those that say I shouldn't have don't have the feel for the court system I do. . . . Also flashing on lawyer's break-ins under Nixon's plumbers. Gerry Lefcourt's in particular, in *Rolling Stone*. That writer might do a good piece on the case.

I was going to try to write the review and do tape—started and drifted off into reveries and distractions. Vigorous correspondence with you is needed. My brain is decaying. I crave ideas that probe and I'm surrounded by recipes for tuna surprise.

Everything coming up sad today, even the fact that Gerald Ford has a golden retriever for a dog.* The weather's brisk. Fall and Halloween just ain't gonna be the same without you and junior. Hope your spirits are high, and your dope supply adequate. It won't be long 'til we see each other. I'm getting excited, are you?

Sorry I sound a little gray . . . I'm probably doing better than if I was moping around New York with the old gang, though. I don't face boredom at least. So consider this something of a fan letter and at least one copy of the *Voice* got bought this week just to read your piece. Love to the Katzenjammer Kid.

> your friend,
> celery, green but firm.

* We used to have a golden retriever.

Dear Hon!

Have you read *Fear of Flying?* It's definitely an inspiration. I think she's the first woman writer I actually liked reading. No, let me see, I liked *Play It as It Lays* a lot and a little Carson McCullers and Shirley Jackson's short stories. Joan Didion's *Slouching* was also good. . . . Is Plath worth reading? *Fear of Flying* brought me very close to you. All the sexual groping and intellectualizing. She's a hero for getting it all down so crisply. Bravery demonstrated is of more value than bravery explained.

I'm alone in a strange room. Angel is away. Do you really think I'm in love with Angel? Maybe the word gets tossed around from time to time. We're an interesting couple. The only thing we have in common is boldness toward life. She's not an optimistic sort though. Thinks we're put on earth to suffer. She's self-educated, you know, been around the world traveling alone, speaks four languages, drives a motorcycle, truck or horse. We take on the neighborhood teenagers in basketball. She's a very heavy dude. I'm not sure where love, admiration, friendship and sexual desire begin and end these days. I don't think I'm the most detached observer of this situation. It's much safer for me to be with someone though. I've wondered many times if you two would hit it off. Objectively it sounds yes because you're both so interesting, but something in me says no, these things don't work out that way. She, by the by, only thinks in terms of temporary relationships but she's a little shook by all this. I'm the first male who accepts her and doesn't feel compelled to knock her off her pedestal. Then there's her motherly instincts. I mean I'm absolutely the world's worst fugitive and she sees herself protecting me. She says there's no competition with you since she primarily knows me as a different person. She's never once called me by the other name.

Lo luv,

Read your article three or four more times. Making me anxious to see you. Some of your familiar expressions and phrasings brought back old memories. I also like the interview with Liv Ullman by Molly Haskell, who is extremely knowledgeable about films and a good writer. She did that book *Women in the Movies,* didn't she?

Got an old letter, September 12, today. It was nice and general so I could have gotten it any time and enjoyed reading it. It had lots of quotes from women revolutionaries. I was really surprised by that Frenchy Republican chopping up marriage. She must have been incredibly ahead of her time. I guess I told you this but I've not met a single person in these eight or nine months that has anything approaching a feminist position. Neither man, woman, lesbian, intellectual or student. I've met very heavy people. Do you think you are sitting on a New York City phenomenon? Last week I had lunch with an internationally known woman writer. She believed a woman wasn't fulfilled unless she gave birth. Even Angel, for whom I have nothing but respect, is pretty anti-feminist although I've affected her thinking somewhat. Convincing her that she sees things slightly different since she's probably among the most beautiful women in the world. She's no fluffy lightweight either. She's worked to support herself all her life and never relied on a man for anything. Abhors marriage. Very strong in every conceivable way. Got integrity too. She believes though, in a double standard. Expects men to fool around but not women. Some gobbledegook about emotional commitment needed for sexual enjoyment on the part of women. She doesn't believe in all the experimentation stuff and says fooling around cuts the magic out of a relationship. I was about to argue but said, hey, I'm not going to lay out positions just to hear myself yap . . .

She admired your article. I don't know how I got off on this track. It's just that she's in my life and I wouldn't feel right never mentioning her.

Any good gossip? I have none. I am gossip-gutted. I wish I could write something inspiring, this being the seventh anniversary of Che's death, but you do that better than me at this point. I just peed and am going to cook dinner. Asparagus omelet with Gruyère. I think if I were there I'd be doing a book on househusbandry—you know, recipes, sewing, vacuuming, etc. Stuff I don't know but could research. I think I could pull off the right style and even come up with loads of shortcuts. I know cooking is 50 percent presentation, 25 percent good tools, 25 percent good ingredients and the rest imagination. If I go broke I'd like to get a job as an assistant pastry maker in a fancy bakery. It's tough, though, I think it's all unionized. Oh, mundane fantasies.

Wish I were cooking this omelet for you and the kiddo. You should tell him a lot about me cooking for him so he won't grow up prejudiced against it.

So long for now . . . your permanent floating crap game.

The Chattanooga Choo-choo.

Dearest,

No word from you since October 22, which I assume is really October 2, unless you're into time travel as well, and who knows, with you.

So, you are no longer alone! I have to sort out my feelings: a little envy, no jealousy. Is the one you live with a heavy? I mean, do you love her?

I am a little spooked by other things. They are still looking for you. I was with a guy in the country last spring when we were harassed by the cops and the FBI out there. He was forced to show his license to prove he wasn't you. Just this week he told me the feds visited the farm he used to live on in Illinois. His old girlfriend, who lives there now, was pretty suprised, considering she hasn't seen him in months and had never met you.

The *Voice* article attracted *Newsweek* which ran a photo of me and the kid in the "People" section. Wow. It's weird to be in *Newsweek* and at the same time in this cruddy apartment with nothing really changed. Strange contrasts in this life.

Right now I'm working on a long-overdue article on prison families for *Ms.* magazine. Meantime I'm hoping to get a contract for a book giving practical welfare information and organizing techniques. That way I can earn money to live on and continue to organize. I would prefer to visit you after I get the book contract. Then I'll be sure of having enough money. December may be too early. What about January?

I, too, eat yogurt every day for lunch. I'm learning about nutrition so we can stay healthy on our subsistence budget. I had been feeling lousy and realized it was because I was starving. Now I chug-a-lug brewer's yeast every morning and take vitamins and calcium pills. The yeast tastes yukky, to use the kid's favorite word, but I'm glad I've taken this step.

I'm getting more aggressive with men, by the way. It's an amusing adventure because I think I'm really trying to learn how to flirt, and I'm a disaster at it. However it makes me giggle and I would rather giggle than think about the rent.

I'm flying. I just did a cable TV show—fifty minutes of me and two other welfare mothers I invited. We came on angry, and people liked the show. I think it was the best I've done so far. I was prepared and had loads of info.

I'm learning so many new skills lately, but I think what's really happening is I'm learning about freedom. I understand in new ways what you're about and how you got there. I am reminded that you *became* what you are. Becoming is the secret, huh? I think I'm just arriving at the place you were when we met. The more I do what I believe in, the more I start to believe in our equality. It has to do with seeing life more as a process than a series of stages.

The TV show was Sunday night and I sat around the pad all day Saturday wondering how I would pay the rent, considering hooking and suicide, and knowing I couldn't do either. But eventually I got it into my head that was what the TV program should be about, that I must keep channeling the hatred against the powers responsible and not myself, or the kid, or you.

I'm not satisfied yet, though. More to learn.

For almost a year I've met only people whom, under other circumstances, I would never never encounter. I've heard jokes I feel are ridiculous, political views no one would ever voice in front of me. I've walked down side roads of life. "L.A. too much for the man, he couldn't make it . . . so he's leaving the life he's come to know. . . ." And it's all true and goddamn it, I've made it. Fuck it all. I'm free. I ain't going back never— never. What's left now that Max's is closed. A moment in space, a chance to share a moment of witty conversation with William Irwin Thompson, whose *Passages About Earth* I just completed. He's the only one (well, one of a few) who understands what's happening and what's going to happen. I strongly recommend it. He and Erica Jong. Nice couple. Hey, I'm guessing Jong is penning your thoughts and attitudes. Am I correct?

Faith in the future and no regrets for the past. The next trip lurks in the darkened hallway.

What's going on in the world? Israel must be negotiating with the Palestinians secretly. I'd bet my yarmulke and hash pipe on it. I sense the lull. They are both cagey fellows, I can't see any trust at all. This is going to blow soon. France just revaluated her gold currency way upward, of course. Very important because the U.S. might follow to stabilize the monetary situation. This is tantamount to war on the Arabs. It works like this: the Arabs get paid for oil in money revaluated at $42 per ounce, gold on the free market is valued at $180 per ounce, so all of a sudden a buck is worth four times its value. To the Arabs four times less though. As least that's how I understand it. They have no choice but to fight gold with oil.

What a battle. It's great to see an old-fashioned economic war again, fuck ideology. They're gonna fight for money, all bets covered. I sense apocalypse. You have to dig that the last thirty years have seen the U.S. battle ideology, hot and cold war; now it's a new enemy really, an economic rival. There are forces seriously challenging U.S. hegemony in the economic globe. Russia and China never did that. The Arabs, the Japanese and nationalization movements in Third World countries are a serious challenge to the U.S. I'm sure there are generals in the Pentagon who've been thinking this way for a long time. Every time Kissinger insists they'll never use force in the Mideast he's fronting for a war build-up. I sense it. What do you expect from a country whose fifth most admired man in the world is, get this, Richard Nixon. Kissinger's first, Billy Graham second, Rockefeller, Ford and Nixon are the top five. America First, remember. . . .

LaBelle is a super group. Do you like? "We're Just an All-Girl Band" is revolutionary. It's a great song on all levels. It's my favorite of theirs, not "The Revolution Will Not be Televised," which is too obvious and a steal of a poem by Giovanni, I think. Not sure. But "All-Girl Band" is terrific. They are original, truly, and now sports fans, Socialism has some new long-ball hitters and a solid bullpen. They might go all the way when the fall season opens. That is if the Yankees' Jim Hunter doesn't drop the big bomb. Wow. Israel is going to use the first nuclear weapon. Oy gevalt!!

I feel like this should be a love letter but there's so much to tell you that I've not written. I'm doing so much.

Today I saw our old friend Linda. Good conversation. She gave me some good advice. We talked about a conference coming up and I told her about my plans to establish a welfare advocate center. She warned me not to slide into reform, but I told her, no sweat. I ain't working on this project to be a social worker for the rest of my life. It's a way of reaching into the community and drawing together poor women. We will provide welfare counseling and represent people at fair hearings, but our real services will be educational. The goal is not only to help families on a case-by-case basis, but to create an environment in which women who feel helpless can begin to take control over their lives. I believe in organizing people around their needs, something I'm not sure the left agrees with. I told Linda my style might be different from hers but I thought we shared the same anti-imperialist, communist perspective, although I can barely pronounce those two words.

I hope I'm not boring you dear, but I'm trying to learn how to become an organizer of the grass-roots variety. Meanwhile I'm looking for ten to twelve other hardy souls willing to train as welfare advocates with me. I've got a few mothers already but am looking for more.

I am ashamed of the radio show I did and hope you didn't hear it, although I realize that's cowardly, vain and selfish of me. My most important guest canceled one hour before the show and I had to ad lib the entire first hour, when I had had a minute-by-minute schedule planned. So I was awkward and felt ill-informed, and the first hour is the worst. Please don't criticize the show. Criticism from you is unbearable because I believe you. The parts I liked best were the music and the story by Lynda Schor from her book, *Appetites*.

I am stunned by the picture of my two favorite people in *Newsweek*. I've studied it for hours. It is a great picture. The composition and lighting are terrific. The contrast between you (real woman) and Cher (staged phony) and junior (vivacious toughie) and Prince Charles (aristocratic snob) are incredible. Every quote is perfect. Zero criticism, only admiration. More thoughts: You are in such a good position to organize welfare mothers. It's an organizer's dream come true. I love you and your hectic future. I salute you! I want to share with you ideas and clues. Media is the weapon. Media is everything. There's no difference talking to the kid or NBC-TV, everything is media. Practice very hard how to say things. You'll quickly see information breaks down into less than twenty questions, half of which occur every time. Don't waste a breath. Go over in your mind answers to each question, over and over and write out answers. Read literature in the area, learn only what you need to do your job, which is namely to be a "conveyor of information," one who knows through study, practice and most of all Experience. I'm never certain how good a teacher experience is, but the American illusion is that it can't be beat. "I've been there" is equal to two degrees on the subject. Cold-bloodedly throw your and america's bodies into the fight. You are instruments of change. It is the best life anyone could wish. Use the kid as you would use a gun. Fight for the millions of kids and mothers that don't have your chance. I envy you.

Read the *Newsweek* thing carefully. Don't think "It's not the same as a college lecture, it's only a few lines." Marlboro sells billions of cancer sticks based on a few lines. Read a lot of facts but boil them down. Make a list of the ones you need. Use only those that fit your gut emotion whether they come from *Prairie Fire, Ms.* or Rockefeller. Use everything to fight. Get ready for infighting. Accept it as a fact of life. Disarm your opponents with "What the fuck do you know, the only thing you ever stand in line for in America is to hear bullshit lectures like this. Try standing in line to eat!" Heavy, hon.

The U.S. government uses welfare and daytime television the way the Romans used bread and circuses, to keep the poor in line and distracted. It's nothing to do with human kindness. You should consider more exposure. You are right to postpone our meeting. Very right. Fuck the work for the defense committee. The best defense is a good offense.

Don't get into this "I'm embarrassed to be on radio . . . etc." You'll spook yourself out of confidence. Hey, look, I had nothing but guts going for me. White male, too old, wrong background, not enough degrees or too many. Not a pot to piss in. You're smarter than I am. I always felt that. The whole trick is to walk faster with stiffer strides, attuned to everything around you. Engaged! It's not fanaticism, it's just being alive and alert.

RSVP from the coast of North Dakota. Eat 'em up!

Hi honey,

Let's see, what's the gossip. Jerry [Rubin] was in New York and just sold his new book. Fred is drifting around the city, depressed as usual. I bump into him in the street and he came over once or twice. I suspect he liked being in a home, but I never know how to cheer him up and am usually busy making beds or writing outlines when he pops in. All his friends are worried about him but no one knows what to do.

I've been seeing a lot of lefties lately. They are such a unique breed I am intrigued and repulsed simultaneously. Sometimes I can barely understand their sentences. They speak like textbooks. But I keep coming back because I thirst for a dialogue of ideas. This is still the city of a million factions!

Linda had asked me if I was a socialist and I gulped and said, "a communist, really." But recently I've been reading Murray Bookchin, and have become curious about anarchism again. In *Post-Scarcity Anarchism* Bookchin presents, in a systematic way, the ideas and visions we shared in the sixties. His book was published in 1971 but for some reason I don't think you've read it, although you've said many of the same things he does. He says, "We believe that Marxism has ceased to be applicable to our time not because it is too visionary or revolutionary, but because it is not visionary or revolutionary enough. We believe it was born in an era of scarcity and presented a brilliant critique of that era, specifically of industrial capitalism, and that a new era is in birth which Marxism does not adequately encompass and whose outlines it only partially and one-sidedly anticipated. . . . We shall argue that in a more advanced stage of capitalism than Marx dealt with a century ago, and in a more advanced stage of technological development than Marx could have clearly anticipated, a new critique is necessary, which in turn yields new modes of struggle, of organization, of propaganda, and of lifestyle."

I've been reading a lot of theoretical and economical material, trying to map out a nice vision of utopia to hold in my head, even if never get to use it! I'm constructing the dreams, I guess, with which I'll measure reality. Economics is my favorite subject and I never dreamed, never dreamed, I would say that. My father had an M.A. in economics and that always seemed terribly dull to me, sort of like his work, business. But now I remember that he was studying economics in the thirties at N.Y.U. and he considered himself "to the left." When I read the financial pages sometimes I wish he could see me. Maybe he would think "at long last she's into something Substantial!"

Anyway I took the kid to a lefty meeting (where he was, as usual, the only child) and as luck would have it, someone starts reading aloud from one of those fine-print rhetorical tracts so popular with the academic young left. The voice drones on and I start planning tomorrow's schedule: whether I can get from the Lower East Side to Columbia University in a half-hour and if I'll have time to get the laundry and do grocery shopping before picking up the kid at school; it depends on whether I use the Grand Union or the Pioneer, which is closer, but more expensive. All of a sudden I hear the kid's loud voice, "I miss my daddy. I want my daddy." I was very surprised because I've never before heard him refer to you in the presence of strangers. Everybody looked at the kid and was silent, then somebody said, "We'll bring your daddy back after a socialist revolution." We all cheered, some of us with tears in our eyes. The kid's a real show-stopper! Incredible timing, huh? He was totally spontaneous, of course, but imagine if I could train him to say that on cue!

Talking with him is fun now. He's at the stage where he asks, "Where do balloons come from?" "Where do pancakes come from?"

Well, I should go to sleep now.

No sex for three months. Sometimes I just want to be held, to be close to someone for a moment and forget everything else. I am glad you have that in your life, honey. It doesn't surprise me. You and the little one are very tempting for people to love. Very cuddly.

My project, establishing a Downtown Welfare Advocate Center at the church, is proceeding. The size of what I'm basically single-handedly trying to do amazes me. I found fourteen other mothers who are interested and we had the first meeting yesterday. We'll have another next Sunday. Now I'm busy arranging for us to be given a course on the welfare laws and regulations.

Did I tell you I saw Judy Gumbo and Stew? They came into the City last weekend. She has a terrific mind. I wish I had gotten to know her better back in the sixties; it's a shame so many of us then were unaware of the value of friendship, especially between women. I like learning about Marxism from her because she's not only smart, she's mellow.

The kid's been very preoccupied with you. He discovered your first book lying around. Everyday he drags it over (the binding's now broken) and asks me to tell him the story. He likes the writing on your forehead on the cover and I think he would like to have something written on his forehead (*Free* or *Fuck*?). We go directly to the picture section and examine each picture. His favorite is the Mommy-Daddy-at-the-Pentagon one. He likes the Uncle Sam hats we are wearing and your bare chest and beads. Of course he always sees the back photo, too, which is of you being busted at the Dean Rusk demonstration in front of the Hilton. I explain the picture to him and he says, "Bad cops. Cops are bad." He really wants to visit your house. He wants you to teach him somersaults. You'd like him. Snotty nose and dirty face. Poor eater. Bad cough.

Yesterday we trekked out to Shea Stadium to see Laura Cavestany's exhibit at the Avant Garde Festival. She had a tent furnished inside like a living room, including a fireplace with a video fire. On an easy chair sat a dummy stuffed to resemble Jerry Rubin, but it's head was a small monitor playing a videotape of Jerry speaking. He was "watching" another monitor across the room which shows you cooking gefilte fish and reminiscing about the time we brought gefilte fish to the Spocks. People wandered in and out of the tent while the kid and I sat on the floor in our winter coats listening to you recount this private memory, so long gone.

Tootsie, I feel bad about not wanting to visit you. I want to see you, but the trip worries me. I don't know what more to say.

More dear Emma:

Got your October 18 letter, read three times. The country album was exactly where I'm at. Love Tanya Tucker and Waylon Jennings. Also tape of the kid and you. It's hard to write clearly about tape. After I heard it I went for a walk over to someone's house. There was a get-together. I was foggy thinking of you. The kid's voice echoed in my ears and I started to cry. I had to go into the bathroom where the tears came pouring out. It took five minutes or so, then I was O.K. It felt really strange. I joined the people and no one knew. I felt better—more human when I left the bathroom. It's not bad to realize you love something even if you can't have it.

You have to arrange for December meeting. It looks like it has to be. There is a chance it can be put off but if we let December slide by there could be a very long wait. We could shorten the meeting which may make it easier for you. That's fine with me.

I feel awful the letters are getting so slowed down. No letter received since September 22 is terrible. It's hard since continuity is destroyed. I just went wild over your last letter—October 18.

I was happy to see you met with Linda. You have to compensate for straight Marxist-Leninist thinking at times, but she's extremely intelligent, kind and aware of what's going on.

As to your fear of criticism of your radio show, Balderdash! My notes have been completed. I liked it. You were better than you give yourself credit for, which is always a good sign. You're supposed to like about half the things you do. It's all subjective.

141

Your judgment is about half-right. You don't gut check yourself out of action and you don't coast on past efforts.

What else. I'm rereading letter. I think "Yellow Submarine" and other Beatles songs are better than the nursery-rhyme crap we learned as kids, don't you?

I'm very proud of you, my little activist friend.

I had a flash on writing a *Prairie Fire* review for the *New York Times*. I want to do everything I can to make it a hit. I have nothing but praise for the book. I like Murray Bookchin's book, but *Prairie Fire* is more valuable and instructive. I'm more a communist than an anarchist. You're right, labels don't count but "c" stands for organizing and puts you in league with international groups. "A" has zero meaning, in fact, a negative valence. I think people calling themselves anything but communist is a cop out. Organizing people around their needs is correct but you should remember Saul Alinsky worked on that principle and created stronger racist groups of workers in Chicago. When you are organizing people you are performing a service. For that service they should have to struggle with the fact that you're a person with a philosophy the government tells them to hate. Every single thing in *PF* should be explained to people being organized. Subtly if necessary. Nobody knows the history of America as it is taught in *PF*. For example, the poor should be armed with a philosophical basis for why everything is coming down on them. It will make them stronger fighters.

More, more, more. The way we meet will be very simple. Don't sweat it now. I'm sure I'll get nervous about meeting. I am now. It has nothing to do with security. It has to do with feelings toward you and that other life. I'm afraid I might just realize that life is not complete without you or junior. I think I'm on another course and can handle anything, but the crying breakdown naturally got to me and dredged up deep feelings. He and I can't be together and it doesn't matter what sort of pleasure and happiness I experience. I can never know him—and it hurts. I never hide it from myself or Angel or you.

I'm starved for folks with ideas. I'm in with a strange group of people, including some who think Nixon got roasted by the press. Most of my "friends" are older people.

What else, I have a sort of hang-dog look and my hair is a constant problem. There were hysterical sessions with me and Lady Clairol. Once I aimed for blond and ended up gray. Then I'd go red for some time. The thing is, you can't change unless you move, or you have a lot of explaining to do.

The first moment of contact for us is going to be the strangest moment in our lives.

I went to see the fight. Just ecstatic about the outcome. Ali has always been my favorite all-time athlete. I bet on him again. I won when he beat Sonny Liston and was a heavy underdog, and again, now. The only time I saw him fight in the flesh, he lost. He's terrific. What a great idea to bring the fight to Africa. I wonder what he'll do with his life. He probably has more things going for him than anyone on earth, excepting maybe Mao. If Nixon dies it'll be the greatest news double bill in world history. Poor fucker, huh? Two and a half billion people in the world are cheering for him to die. That's gotta be some kind of record. The theater was wild for Ali. I haven't seen so many happy people since Nixon quit.

Did you actually say, "I'm making a life of my own, I don't have time for him?" Zooooowie! I think we need a letter rest. I'm having wicked dreams. I'm flooded with flashbacks. I thought I saw Ed Sanders on the street the other day.

Hope you can benefit from all comments on the radio show. I really liked it. I hope you don't slow down your activity. I can't understand the blow-up. O.K., let's get it on.

 See you in the Great Divide. Your favorite midge,
 David Cassidy

By the 7th I will decide a date for the December visit. My head is not into all the preparation necessary. I never have time to plan it and I still have no money. I honestly am not eager to visit you in December. I am in the middle of projects here. Also I don't know the purpose of a visit anymore. I don't think anything new will be decided. I love you but I don't see myself moving in with you unless my tiny world here collapses. I have not earned the right to be a fugitive yet and I don't want to be one. Maybe the time is not right to be with you. Coming in December means dropping the only project I care about. It is a shame that your present situation places so many burdens on me and others who love you. Oh, I know in my heart it is unfair to blame you for having been a devoted revolutionary. It's just that the oppressors really have gotten us down. They are more to blame than any of us. I am crying. Because I see no solutions to my problems, or to yours, or to ours. You and the kid are the only ones I've ever loved. We'll work it out. I'll come.

Went to a party with the old gang tonight at the Chelsea, but had to leave early because the sitter expected me. Frances is back in town but off to London next week. She looks terrific.

The FBI has been making new rounds, I heard.

Jerry told me he had trouble finding a publisher for his new book although he ended up with a good deal. He says the publishers have an active hatred against you and him, that to them you both represent Violence. His new book is very personal and psychological. It's his seventies head, he says, but the publishers won't let him change, they won't let him grow out of his sixties stereotype. He was upset and surprised, but I knew all this from your troubles trying to get *Book of the Month Club* published.

Gus was also at the party. He's going to the West Coast and is considering entering electoral politics. He thinks we should make demands for full employment. We argued. He says we could have full employment rebuilding slums and doing the good work America needs done. I agree in concept but I don't trust how the system would implement the reality, just as with guaranteed income. I think the government would have showcase projects of "good works," but force most poor people to work at slave wages for private industry or the war machine. I would love laying bricks if I thought it would improve my living conditions but more likely I would end up hunched over a sewing machine working on the latest fall-apart acetate dress style. In fact I once considered applying for a job in one of the neighborhood loft factories, but I learned only garment piecework is available for women and the wages are so low I could never afford daycare. The idea had appealed to me because I could walk to work. In Chinese communes the workplace, the daycare facilities and the public dining hall are within

145

walking distance from the home. Life would actually be easier for me in that poor country than it is here, in the richest one.

The economic situation is very frightening. The poor here are being squeezed unmercifully by inflation, and no one's making a peep. The National Welfare Rights Organization just closed its office in Washington, and no longer exists. It couldn't pay its bills. The movement must start all over again from the grass roots and it will take time. In the Great Depression there was massive unemployment and intense suffering in the early years but no attempts were made to give relief until massive disorder and unrest spread throughout the country. Then Roosevelt saved capitalism by a series of emergency relief measures and reforms which culminated in the Social Security Act. I wonder if guaranteed income could emerge as the major reform this time around. There is already widespread dissatisfaction with the present welfare system and talk of extending unemployment benefits indefinitely. However, it has to be remembered that Nixon himself had a guaranteed income package which allocated $2,500 a year to a family of four. *Adequate* income would be an improvement but it wouldn't change the class structure or smash imperialism because it doesn't call for the redistribution of wealth, or power, only a bigger sop to those at the bottom. Some liberals would combine guaranteed adequate income with meaningful tax reform. Do you think this system is infinitely flexible and can always adjust with reforms to save itself, or can it be broken? Or will it just disintegrate under its own decadence? I don't really know why I ask you, you always go for broke!

Darling I'm sad at the feds still visiting people and sad if you must be a fugitive forever. Incredible that the pigs have the power to inflict that kind of sadness. I repress the totality of it almost always. What they have done to us fills me with such anger that I can only find satisfaction in working to defeat them.

Dear,

I cannot visit you. I'm sorry. The thought of it tortures me so I am trying to wrestle with the demon and write this letter and clear it up.

I do not know all the motivations, only some:

1. I have no money and worry about it a lot.
2. The responsibility of this trip. I cannot bear the thought that I might lead them to you and might fuck up. Although I don't yet know where I'll be going.

I can't do it.

I have no more strength. I cannot fulfill my responsibilities to you. At least not the trip.

This is my second version of this letter but it is still hysterical. Please don't be angry with me. Have compassion. I can hardly manage anymore. Try to get others to help you as much as possible.

I simply cannot come. Please understand and forgive me if you are pissed. I can't handle it. My hands are full. I can only take on so much. Right now I can't even pay next month's rent.

Today the hearings in the case started. Hearings on a motion to throw the case out on the basis of illegal wiretapping.

We have an affidavit from the super of my mother's building which states: (1) both cops visited the building several times, (2) one of them talked with a doorman, in addition to the super, (3) one was seen coming from the direction of the apartment, (4) a long-haired cop with headphones was seen at the basement phone board of the building for five hours one afternoon, (5) the super let the cops into the apartment, where they stayed for a half-hour; one of them spending five minutes in the bedroom behind a closed door, (6) the super gave the cops a duplicate key to the apartment. This all occurred in May or June, 1973.

When the super took the stand today he agreed to everything he had previously sworn to except the parts about giving the cops a duplicate key and letting them into the apartment. He is not a U.S. citizen and appears very scared. The cop who testified today denied that he has ever been to the building. He admitted meeting with the police informer since June 1, but denies your name was ever mentioned between them until the day before the bust, August 27. One of our leads is freezing up and it looks suspicious to me, as though the guy has changed his mind because he's scared.

Ron Rosenbaum is covering the hearings for the *Voice*. Everyone who attends is fascinated. There are two completely contradictory stories emerging—and you have to determine who's lying, who's telling the truth. The super has no reason whatever to lie, the cops have every reason, but I don't know if we can convince the judge.

The other cop took the stand today and he, too, denied ever visiting either building or mentioning your name to the police informer. Desi, the superintendent in my mother's building, is obviously intimidated by the cops, by the judge, by the whole scene, but he insists he saw the cops in the building. The judge told him he was in trouble for denying what he had previously sworn to (giving the cops a duplicate key and letting them into the apartment), and ordered him to get a lawyer to protect himself.

We've had two meetings of the advocate center group and are starting our training course next week. We'll be located at the church, which is a real community crossroads. Things are looking good, but it all depends on the team I've assembled. The next step is to go after funding. Applying to foundations seems an elaborate method to get a phone line for our office but I see no other way. None of us can afford to pay dues and I don't know any wealthy patrons. I've been working hard and the only encouragement is the progress of the project itself, yet step by step it's moving toward reality.

Sunday the kid and I visited Jill and Terry at their loft. They may be my first clients, which would be a great way to start, helping friends. I'm learning the welfare regulations and collecting loads of statistics. Forty-five percent of all women who are separated are below the poverty level in this country.

I have a meeting here in a few minutes so I will sign off now and continue next week after Monday's hearings.

What if I become as egomaniacal as you? There are indications it's happening. When we get together we'll both talk about ourselves for hours, not listening to the other!

We had a nice Thanksgiving dinner at Trucia's and Jerry's house, even Mother was there. She came to New York to see all of us, but most of all junior, whom she misses constantly. The FBI has been bothering her again, but she's refused to see them. I feel kind of bad telling her the material coming out in the hearings about her apartment. She must imagine the building staff sneaking around, gossiping about her behind her back while she was living there, leading her normal, innocent life. And she has to bear everything alone, like your mother. She worries about the kid and me, and I try to reassure her but I don't know if I succeed. She might take us to Radio City Music Hall tomorrow, and she's offered to babysit Saturday night so I can attend a party Jay is giving before he returns to Europe. Mother wants to go out to the cemetery Sunday, so Penny is lending us her car.

The holidays are turning into a little vacation which I hadn't expected. We played a Pinocchio film for the kids this afternoon and when Pinocchio is reunited with his daddy, all the grownups secretly thought of a certain three year old who was watching, and his daddy.

It will happen one day, when the time is right.

High hon,

Sad movie on the late show tonight. Couple couldn't get it on, killed their kid in the process. It's 2 A.M. I generally go to sleep early, rise early. Tonight was different. I've been trying not to think of you and junior for a week which is like trying not to think of the proverbial elephant. Lots of letters have crossed my mind. The one when I go far away and never see you again. The one to end the correspondence drifting in aimless scratches with a swift blow, painful at first, but good for the long haul.

Are you still into meeting? I guess we have time to figure it out. My feeling is it won't come off. It's been put off three or four times. I think I smell male pride bristling behind my liberated ears.

The above was written a week ago. Today arrived your November 11 scratchings about not coming. That's fine with me. I sensed it coming a long time ago, and it has nothing to do with money or wigs. But I feel much the same way.

You seem pretty disoriented in your last letters, the most depressed ever. I'll tell you now you can forget forever any "responsibility" to me. I mean it. In point, this I hope will terminate our communications. I'm not angry. I just smell being scapegoated for "failures" perceived as coming. I'm not going into the past. Paradise is coming to an abrupt end for me too. The place, I mean. I'm going away and do not think it wise to correspond. I get ample reports on the kid's well-being and in the back of my mind know someday it'll be right for us to meet.

151

I would like you to play no role in the defense committee. In some way explain to junior I'm never coming back. I couldn't make a tape for junior because I couldn't go on perpetuating the myth of the nuclear family reunited in never-never land.

I don't want to take issue with you on any points you raise. I'm not into doing battle, analyzing or much of anything. In time we'll tell everything differently. My current life affects the way I view the past, same as you.

I think the tone and manner of this letter is a reaction to your "I'm sorry" letter.

Before you decide to have the nervous breakdown suggested in your last letter let me say this. Quite definitely I offer to take the kid. It's quite possible, given the nature of my lifestyle (homebody and exciting travel). I'm not kidding. Angel says it's O.K. and we'd manage. The reorientation would take only a few months. The technical problems of being with the kid are less and less as I become more sure of myself. It would, of course, have to be for a long period.

The money talk and letters to my mamma are a traditional way to make divorced husbands feel guilty. Someday I'll write a list of suggestions for ex-husbands to make their wives feel guilty. Stuff like offering to take kids, etc. Lots of heavy quotes from *Les Misérables* with hunks of bmroken glass when the Male Chauvinist Pig cuts his hand grabbing the loaf of bread.

Ah, you'll figure it all out . . . how men never get the emotional chance in life to write "I'm having a nervous breakdown."

You've come a long way, baby. Don't blow it.

Thanks for the words, and goodbye.

Darling:

It is strange. I'm sitting here on my bed in my usual spot, smoking a joint, trying to take in some pleasure before the day ends. It's 2 A.M. and the kid is tucked away in bed, fast asleep. For some reason (maybe because I'm happy) my mind flew back over the past seven years of our marriage and I saw patterns, I saw meaning and growth, where I had only previously seen confusion—at least on my part. It's as though, looking back, I can read my subconcious. I hope you will be honored by my honesty and not angry. It is because I love you that I want to be honest.

I remember an acid trip we took in 1967 in our St. Marks Place apartment, when I questioned whether we were both on the same trip, or should be. By that time I couldn't keep up with all your activities and wasn't sure I wanted to. I didn't know if I should work with you politically or go my own ambivalent way. I finally decided, not without reluctance, that I was a separate person and I gradually withdrew from your activities.

The spring before the Chicago Convention Susan and I got into stringing hippie necklaces with those teensy weensy beads, remember? I used to sell them to the stores on Bleecker Street for twelve dollars a dozen. Susan and I became addicted to beading and could never stop. Once we were both crouched over the bead table, our eyes glassy, our circulation at a standstill, when one of us tried to get up and couldn't. We both fell back on the cushions and giggled hysterically, tears streaming out of our eyes, knowing it was time to give up beading. By then I was planning to join you in Chicago, anyway. As you wrote in your first book, we went our separate ways, for the most part, during the convention.

153

After the convention our closest friends moved to country communes and you were nationally known and much sought after. Our disparity in the eyes of the world grew, and if I was jealous I hid it from myself, but I was uneasy, unsure. Not knowing what role to play I tried to lose myself in sewing, embroidery, crocheting and cooking. Then, practically out of the blue, I was offered a contract for a novel and I was ecstatic because the publisher was willing to publish it under a pseudonym. The Chicago conspiracy indictments came down just as I was starting work on the book, and I decided to remain in New York while you went to Chicago for the trial. Well, once the trial started I couldn't resist being drawn to it, like everyone else. It was the most exciting event of the times, and I could have a ringside seat. It seemed more meaningful and dramatic than any work I was doing, and of course, my work suffered as a result.

In the months following the trial I stupidly relinquished further responsibility for the book by not overseeing its publication. Instead I went to Europe with you and ended up visiting Tim Leary and Eldridge Cleaver in Algeria. By the time we came back I was disillusioned with the movement and finished with the book. No one believed what I said about Cleaver although subsequent events proved I was right, and years later others on the trip apologized to me. I was vaguely unhappy in this period, without direction, and lonely, although I didn't realize I was lonely. You were less in love with me then, but I wasn't aware of that either. While you were doing time in Cook County jail for having written FUCK on your forehead, I was overjoyed to discover I was pregnant. We both wanted the kid, but I remember once when we fought you said I wanted to have a child because I was bored. I hated you for saying that but now I understand what you meant. Yes, I do, hon. There was a grain of truth in it: I had copped out on my book and felt like a failure; having a child seemed an easier dream to fulfill.

Really, it's not so easy, as I have discovered! Right after the baby was born you were hit with an incredible number of problems: you had to do the speaking tour to pay the IRS $9,000 in taxes on money you turned over to the Chicago defense committee; there were lawsuits over *Steal This Book;* and you were suddenly the object of personal attacks in the press, many of which were a reaction to *Steal This Book.* I was weak and exhausted from nursing the baby 'round the clock, and I started rebuffing you more and more, sexually. I became conscious of negative feelings toward you and toward myself. It was tempting to blame you for my own mistakes and no doubt I made a few stabs in that direction. At the same time some of my reservations about the women's movement melted. Only in the new wave of feminist literature could I find solace for my private woes, but I was mucho afraid of meeting any feminists in the flesh because I feared they would use me to attack you. Don't forget, by 1971 feuding of the factions had become a lifestyle in itself, no doubt helped along by Cointelpro and Chaos.

Each time you were away and I had to struggle alone with the baby I became more self-reliant. Surviving alone, what's that? But schlepping with the baby and overcoming all obstacles, that's strength. My strength grew slowly and finally asserted itself in the move to the country. I didn't know a soul out there, but I was determined to leave the city with or without you, so I moved out there alone with the kid and fixed up the house. The two of us lived there under a pseudonym, in the middle of the woods, miles from anyone we knew. Looking back, I wonder how I did it but life there was serene and I was happy to make a few friends completely on my own. Then, too, I didn't have to worry about money because you were supporting us. Life was pleasantly slow when you weren't there and when not caring for the child I read and thought a lot, correlating my experiences with those of other women. The fierce man-hating phase I was in for most of the winter abated as spring '73 rolled around. Reluctantly I began fantasizing about affairs with other men. I desired a secret world where I could be a new person, not just with women, but with men.

You started coming out to the country more and more, bringing friends from the city. Thus began my parade of "crushes" on other men which caused so much furious and hilarious confusion that summer. Truly I was The Country Wife. Everyone else in our circle, including you, had been fucking around for years when I emerged from my cocoon and stumbled into the game, breaking all the rules. God, how those infatuations embarrass me now! You were jealous and wouldn't admit it, and I was selfish and wouldn't admit it. But we kept trying to work things out between us. I think we could have, but CRASH. The bust happened. Suddenly you were locked in the Tombs, facing life imprisonment. Your freedom had to be the first priority and our plans for building a new lifestyle together had to be postponed indefinitely. With great agony we decided to separate, unsure how or when we would see each other again. It's so painful and scary to risk change, but so goddam exciting. We made the right decision.

I see my life in Technicolor and I needed to learn I could see it that way without you. I can't regret the past either, because now I understand how it brought me to this moment. Yet how blind we always are in the present!

What's the next thing that's gonna shake us up? Children's liberation? To occur when we meet in Sumatra in 1980, or Berkeley? Or tomorrow, when the kid wakes up?

Maybe when we meet we will each be polygamous. Maybe we will work out a new kinship system based on friendship which will rival whatever the Samoans or the Kwakiutls had! Anything is possible. Like you, I enjoy inventing it as we go along. Our invisible family already transcends time and space.

WARNING! VERY HEAVY PSYCHOLOGICAL INFO
IN THIS LETTER

Hello again—

Can we just talk? I've been reading Carlos Castaneda's *Tales of Power*. I like his four books very much, and I don't know if I told you in a past letter, but sometimes I try some of the exercise trips Don Juan is into. Like crossing your eyes and playing with the images until you produce two steady ones. So I'm lying in bed working on another one: the task of finding your hands in a dream. I had never tried it before. It's really interesting. See, the object is to relax yourself first, lower all your defenses to the extent you can, get very little in your mind and climb over these walls until you are able to penetrate your dream world. Enter it with a reality equal to the other reality that's you the dreamer.

Tonight I got a peek and sort of panicked a little. I started to go under quickly, which I know from autohypnosis sessions, and just let my mind float. (I was wishing I had some Indian sitar music and really saw for the first time why that music is so good for the internal trip. How voices singing would be distracting. How orchestra instruments would compete for your attention. A sitar is the only instrument you can listen to for a long long time and not get bored or jarred.) So next I tell myself a joke which is, "I'll have no trouble finding my hands, they're generally down around my crotch scratching my nuts." And I chuckled because it's not only a good personal joke but a good joke, period. Then I remind myself that I'm

157

doing all this intellectualizing and joking to distract myself
from going in and I get rapidly very deep and honest with
myself. Move to different break. I mean sometimes it seems
like teleportation, definitely a physical sensation. Sooooo anyways, my mind moves to a deeper level. And I found myself
engaged in dialogue with myself.

"Who do you want to be?"

"I don't know. Give me some roles to play and I'll see
when I play them if I like'em enough to be'em."

"Be crazy," I shout.

I started to act crazy in my dream or if not the dream on
the way to the dream, the dream in which I would try to find
my hands. After a while I get confused and panicky. I think I
started yelling, "I'm crazy! I'm crazy!" Then I got scared
'cause I felt I was on such a level of consciousness that "I"
could have convinced myself, and not knowing my dream world
from my "real" world, I might not find my way back and would
be, as I have been enculturated to believe, "crazy." So I
popped down another road, stopping only to "congratulate"
myself for venturing that far, concluding (or deluding) that I
was far from crazy and actually some sort of god for even
having the strength to see that vision.

The dialogue began again and I questioned, "What do you
want in life?" I quickly answered, "I want to travel," and I
do. So I concluded quickly that I'm going to start doing that
right away. I further conclude I'm pretty happy so I must be
getting what I want out of life. Then I try harder and run
down the list. Do you want to be in love? Do you want to be
famous? Do you want to have people listen when you speak?
What do you want that you can't have? And I said, "I want to
see the kid." And I said, "Wow, I do." I really do. And I
can't. And then realized that probably is the first frustration
I've ever experienced in my life. The first sort of compromise
between desire and reality I ever had to work out on this level.

I really don't think anything like that ever happened to me before, and I wondered if that was the human experience lots of folks always talk about.

Soooo I try some more and I'm really pondering about how I always got what I really wanted in life and still do except for this one thing. I'm wondering if not getting what you want out of life frustrates a person enough so that they get so weak they go nuts—or neurotic. And I think, obviously, yes. So I wonder if I'm down the road and does this mean some sort of defense mechanism, say a personality change or a strange rash will occur. Oh goodie, I think, wonder what it'll become. Then I conclude that getting what I want for so long, like early mother warmth, just is heaps of pluses and in my arrogant optimism realize I'm one of the few nonneurotic people I'll ever come across.

I think unhealthy people (I see more, in my travels, of Middle Americans than in the revolutionary-adventurer world we both used to live in) are people who come out poorly in the little ego stories they tell themselves. Or when they recall the day's events. Something, by the way, that can never let you see your hands in a dream, I'm sure.

I think I always wanted people to listen to what I had to say and to like me. I've pulled that off (twice in different lives before pretty different audiences). Not only do I mean the "group" I'm in as opposed to the "group" I was in, but I even mean the differences between you and Angel. You are as different as I could imagine two human beings to be and still allow me to really like both. I can't discuss her much with you. But I wanted to say that when I told you the story of the Indian Princess and that of Angel you wrote you felt sorry for the Indian Princess. But why no joy for Angel (quite a liberation story)? Let's translate that into revolutionary political terms for a sec. Question: Which are you more of, happy the Arabs united behind the Palestinians or sad about Chile?

I'm trying to think of another example but having difficulty. Something more personal. Let's try: Which are you more of, sad you can't enter into some love relationship or happy you have discovered a new independent you? That sounds O.K., but you know better and could raise questions more properly. As to me, I'm more up on the Arabs than down on Chile.

I think I can do the relationship trip better than you. And you the alone trip better than me. My biggest human fault is not knowing how to live with myself alone.

I'm entering a phase like you are. I've wanted to write progressively less and less and I'm sure the past letters will show some sort of "running out" on things to say and deepness of dialogue. Our relationship, although very beautiful and respected by me, holds me back from entering a new life. More than anything else I can think of. And of course for my survival and my sanity I'm being forced down another road. I just don't mean by the circumstances of my situation either. I mean also by my need to discover the world. Not just the world out there but the one in here also. I think now is a good time to tell you something, well, let me start slow. Without the letters to and from you I would be having letter correspondence with more people as my new self than as my old! I sense a strange sort of schizophrenia when I pick up a pen to write. I've even asked one pen pal whom I was corresponding with under the old identity if I could switch to the new, which would be safer, more honest and actually more fun to hear from. I'm awaiting the answer. Does any of this make sense?

I think you, more than anyone else, can understand this. Well, hold onto your chair. I'm nervous to write this, yet I want to tell you—I'm getting married. Oh God! That's gotta be the strangest thing a guy could tell his wife. Should I have? This is all so confusing. When I was growing up there was nothing that I can recall that suggested I'd become a bigamist. Remember way back when I suggested, after a little philosophical interchange, how if you fell for someone you might try to commit bigamy to make the point about not "*un*-caring" for someone you "care" about? Well, I was already thinking of it as happening to me. This is not just a matter of what if this life collapsed and the other life resumed. Neither the law nor, should I add, myself are going to allow that. I suppose if it did I would try to do some balancing act but I am definitely "coupled," so to speak, and it would not end the day some magic carpet landed in Times Square.

I think with your last letter and this one our relationship has entered a new level of honesty. I'm glad and I hope you are. I hope you get the best of everything in life, but I don't want to go down the guilt drain if you don't. I hope the opposite is true too, you for me, I mean. I'll really be proud if I pull off the transition and proudest of all if we can both in our separate ways keep moving on.

I never wrote such a heavy letter in my life. I suspect the same for your last too.

Thanks for the lift. You really do have some leadership quality.

Love,
Abbie

I wanted to go through everything with you in person but since you're reluctant to come, I guess I have to tell you all this in a letter. Terrible form. We have traveled far in different directions.

Darling,

I have only good feelings and scarcely know how to express them all on such a momentous occasion. Mazel tov! Best wishes for the future!

I still love you and want only your happiness and safety. I am glad you are not alone. On one level I realize I am more alone now than ever, but on another level it's O.K. and I know I can handle it. I also feel we are not finished—although I don't know exactly what that means.

If only I could think of some original lines for this unique situation. I mean, I can't even say "Don't leave your dirty socks lying around the bedroom," 'cause for all I know you do your own laundry now. And then, I'm sorta different too and don't give a fuck anymore about dirty socks.

Magic still exists for us, linking us in new ways. The timing of my letter of the 4th and your wedding announcement just amazes me. Everything you wrote about the old you and the new you is ditto for me. I have felt held back in precisely the same way, writing to you. Only with fear and reluctance did I send you material about what I was actually doing. I'm so glad we leveled wtih each other at exactly the same time.

All those hysterical letters I wrote you were the result of guilt at not visiting you. Whenever I didn't want to accede to a request or demand from you, I've tried to paint my situation in the blackest terms, afraid, I guess, that somehow I would hurt you if I refused your demands out of happiness or independence. I was wrong and stupid. The guilt of not visiting you was so strong I was unable to write except to complain how hard everything was. And the guilt made me resentful toward you.

162

But lately the bad feelings just dissolved. Maybe as a result of your nice interest in what I was doing. I had been afraid that the things I'm really proudest of, somehow, would hurt you because they were exclusive of you. The other night I felt good and suddenly wanted to convey to you more of my new identity, how I saw our years of marriage, and why I felt more positive toward you. It is magic to me that I decided to do this all before I got your letter which tells me that for you it has been exactly the same.

I assume from the way you avoid mentioning Angel too much that you really love her. I think I know how that operates because of my own fantasies or realities with other men, although I haven't fallen in love. The reason I felt sad for the Indian Princess was because she was the loser. Angel (then known as Sphinx) was obviously the winner, although I had no idea then how much she was winning! Since I have been lonely, and I have had romantic disappointments, I identified with Princess.

I have no idea whether Angel and I would get along or not. The only thing I hate about meeting women you like is if I am disappointed. I would rather feel violent hatred or jealousy or love—anything but disappointment. Angel and I could be friends even if we differ on female politics. I wonder if we will get together one day and giggle about you. You give me the impression I'm an oatmeal cookie compared to her petit four. I sort of like being an oatmeal cookie. It's a new experience, although I myself would choose to eat a petit four.

I think part of me hopes that you love her because then maybe I could, and I would never be jealous. The marriage must be good for security, but I can't imagine my hubby would marry for security alone. You don't strike me as the type!

I love you and I'm glad you're married. I don't want anything from you. Not even your love if it's gone. I only want your happiness. I mean it.

Dear one,

Two letters arrived today, one November 27 and the other undated. They both have me confused because they speak of coming to visit. Look, let me state my position. I would like to see you. I would like to see you because I meet very few people who are worth more than casual acquaintance. You're someone I like a lot, we have a lot to discuss when together and I trust you. The "leading them to me" is ridiculous. I worked out route and manner long ago. It's easy. The psychological problems are more threatening, but if you can handle the info I've sent in the letter I wrote last night then there is no great psychological fear for either of us, really. So, whatever you decide or have decided. . . .

I'm pissed they're still looking. What a bunch of bastards. I've become somewhat politically active lately but it's very hard. I'm like a ballplayer who's been in the major leagues and now is asked to play sandlot ball. As soon as I speak I become "leader," noticeable, hence, in danger. Also a taste spurs me to want to go further. Conflict is inevitable. I guess I sense some call to destroy which seems to me some sort of violent death. I view this period as "in-between," and love life too much to hurry the whole nutty business along. I'm back into karate. I study two hours each day so am very body oriented. The PLO has caused me to enter a few debates on the subject, flashing, of course, since most Americans have opinions about as deep as a commercial for Excedrin.

War is imminent in the Mideast. I am violently anti-Israel and no longer believe they have a right to exist. During the past

164

ten years they have forfeited any right they might have "earned." They will strike first, but whether their actions are preemptive or "reactionary" is superfluous, since a state of war has existed between them and the Palestinians since 1947 (and before). Zionism was the cause of the war. The PLO are as guilty of aggressions as were the North Vietnamese!! Pictures of Israeli mothers weeping after a bomb explodes are a nightly feature on the boobtube. Tenfold the number of those wailing mammas are bawling their eyes out in Lebanon from Israeli air raids, but we never see that. The U.S. has always conveniently drawn a distinction between a bomb placed in a building and one dropped from the sky. How convenient and disgusting. I hate Israel and want to see the Palestinians triumph. I know the U.S. is prepared to go to war there.

Ninety-nine percent of the congressmen back Israel and through the media the vast majority of Americans. Meanwhile, judging from the U.N. vote, the rest of the world stands behind the Palestinians. There are many analogies with Vietnam. The greatest nonanalogies, Israeli technological and military superiority to the South Vietnamese, their cultural identity with the West and the irrational sympathy and guilt they muster from W. W. II experience, only force me to conclude they are destined to bring the U.S. into war. I'm amazed at how venomous hatred for the Arabs is among liberals. More among liberals! So Israel, unless it reverses its entire foreign policy and negotiates directly with the PLO, has to choose war and quickly. I think U.S. policy encourages this. Kissinger's hand-holding of Hussein, for example. How idiotic, asking for the Palestinian's natural enemy to negotiate the future of Palestinian land with Israel. Two U.S. puppets. The Arabs have become very sophisticated in military spending as well as global politics and are going to deal very sharply with Israel. There will be missiles fired. Meanwhile, the new government in Portugal is not going to be that hospitable to the U.S. using the Azores to supply

Israel; and the other European powers because of their oil problems are not about to lend a hand. One clearly senses an Israeli determination to get it started. The U.S. wants this. It's always been U.S. policy to support Israeli aggression, to hope that the Arab powers get drained in the fight and hence weaker at the oil-bargaining table. The U.S. eventually has to send troops to help Israel. Picture a six-month struggle, even though Arab casualties are running high, say ten to one the number of Israelis killed. In six months Israel could loose eight thousand troops and civilians if the Arabs used missiles or penetrated the cities with guerillas. Obviously they have that capacity and will. I think the U.S. will quickly enter under the guise of a "peace-keeping force."

There won't be the base for organizing against such a war as with Vietnam, and left protests will be suppressed with a mighty boot. We are not talking about the distant future either. America's future will be decided outside its borders, same as happened with the Roman Empire. That affects what happens internally (Vietnam a prime example). The United States does not exist inside its borders.

If I was active in the old role politically I would already have gone to Israel where I would have debated someone like Kahane right in Jerusalem or whatever place was correct. I would have tried to structure it in such a way that I got thrown out of Israel without being lynched. Then I'd head for Arab countries to learn more. I'd return and begin organizing teach-ins, educational stuff. That's if I were politically active.

I'm flattered that you ask about political views. Honestly. I've been giving Bookchin's book a lot of thought and consider it's philosophy inferior to *Prairie Fire* although rubbing the two together produces more sparks in my head than I've experienced through the printed word in years. The question of identification with the wave of Third World aspirations seems critical. There's a tide moving, challenging U.S. hegemony. It has movements in various stages of development from China to some group of urban fighters in Buenos Aires. Bookchin is not ready to say we stand shoulder to shoulder together. I can't accept post-scarcity politics in a world that suffers from scarcity and I can't understand a revolution that occurs solely in the U.S. where those politics make a lot of sense (on paper anyway) because I'm interested in world revolution and it means sharing the U.S. resources on such a scale that the standard of living experienced by us all is decreased. Sure, eventually post-scarcity politics allow for a meaningful drive toward utopian society. But that's later.

I'm a communist, not an anarchist, and believe in democratic centralism, not small groups working things out for themselves. I'm not anti-Bookchin. His voice is necessary and he's correctly trying to adjust what history has taught him to the American experience. He's like a good architect but he's an architect without engineers. So where's the house? A bunch of asshole Zippie copycats and a few college symposiums? What about the world?

I wrote a whole lot of stuff to you about welfare mothers. I'm not happy with them. You'll get ideas as you get into it. The creative aesthetics of organizing are the easiest part. The most difficult is finding people you respect and can work with. You should try to collectivize as quickly as you can. You could avoid some mistakes I made. By the time I was open for the collective experience, that is, when I met a group of equals, we were on trial. Tom Hayden squashed the idea of organization building in a story that never got told. We can't afford the indulgence of not arriving at collective consciousness. I, too, have great respect for Judy Gumbo. She's an excellent thinker. I never found anything she ever did or said disagreeable and her thinking is many times more advanced than my own thinking, which is patently naïve at times. Many times.

I used to work with welfare mothers in Massachusetts, fighting for representation of the poor on poverty councils. I made good friends. We made a lot of trouble for the agency, but I don't know the particulars on your turf. I know general principles. Slam the liberals and take their handouts. Get your good people together and talk, talk, talk, about the issues, about what's happening. Slowly some of the turf or scene develops in your head. Your eyes and ears are always open to contacts, phone numbers, a way of reading the papers, watching TV, so that you glean what is relevant for your struggle. You know everything there is to know so that you're quickly attuned to loose ends, contradictions that don't jive, ways to put ideas to work.

You need the type of dedication that says, "I don't care if no one else wants to struggle. I do. I do it for my own well-being." Therefore sixteen hours of stamp licking or envelope stuffing, organizing meetings that don't come off, having a speech go badly, getting beat up, all that work stuff . . . becomes as natural as the weather. You reach a point where every act becomes instinctual. You never complain, only work on your own act and expect nothing from nobody. You never lose your temper. Even your TV anger is "posed." I can tell from letters you write you're getting better.

The interesting stuff is what's happening around me and I can't tell even you, as I've explained. So I have to get philosophical which loses its meat for me and I think gets stagey.

I'm not surprised about the reaction of publishers to Jerry's book. I knew the ballgame was over for me with *Steal This Book*. Every book I wrote (over one million copies sold in all) made money. Three out of three. So it's no sour-apple deal. It's a complicated situation writing revolutionary books for capitalist publishers. Naturally the question of violence comes up. Revolutions happen to be violent affairs. It has nothing to do with how you dress. All that was camouflage. Wolf in hippie sheep clothing. Here's my liberal friend arguing with me about

Israel: "Oh, don't get me wrong, I believe *in principle* with many revolutionary movements in the world. I draw the line at terrorism." I asked him to name a movement that didn't employ "terrorism." He couldn't. "So you like revolutionary movements in the abstract but can't name one of the more than two or three hundred active in the world you approve of." If welfare is cut and babies go without milk, that's clearly violent to me. What's the difference if some "innocent victim" dies of malnutrition or a bomb placed in a hotel. But all this is superfluous.

You do not read my letters and address yourself to each point. It's a great frustration writing to you. I lay out your letters in front and answer each point. I might miss some. Sometimes the letter seems to jump, but I'm answering each point.

I wish we were together. The feelings I have for you can never stop. What can I say, life goes on. I only write to let you know, to keep the honesty we have maintained, to let you "off the hook." I now realize you might decide to come anyway. There's time and my arms are open wide, but don't feel sorry if you don't.

I wander through the path of laughing, dancing children wondering what he looks like. Ask him a few times if he wants to be with his daddy, if he could keep it all a secret and tell no one but you? Maybe if you ain't into coming the kid could. I'll spend as much time with him as you want. It's quite a secure place I'm in and enough room and food. He would have a good time and the risk to me isn't great. I hope he doesn't grow up thinking I don't love him. Naturally I'll pay all expenses for travel or whatever. It's worth everything just to be with him and not lose track of his reality. Think about it. Quickly, I'm not afraid of it.

Hectic day and very tired. Throat hurts. So I will try to make this brief.

There are some good developments in the case. We now have testimony that one of the cops visited Carol's* building three times during the spring and summer preceding the bust, impersonating a telephone company repairman. This means they were watching, tapping or bugging the place you were staying and her apartment for three months prior to the bust. I just wish we had more corroborating evidence. We will never be able to produce the surveillance devices themselves because my mother moved out a few months after the bust, and the apartment was repainted and the phone changed, plus the new tenant will not let our investigator into the apartment to check it out. Besides, who knows what devices they actually use. I saw the movie *The Conversation,* where an investigator goes crazy looking for the bug in his own apartment. We've uncovered a lot, but not the whole thing yet, and time is short. The hearings are coming to an end.

I received your fascinating letter of the 10th today. The reason I never answer your letters point by point is that I usually only read them once. I've been too paranoid to keep them in the house more than a day, so I rarely get the opportunity to reread them at my leisure.

I'm glad you're a commie! I'm further to the left too. Any ideas about the relation of communism to guaranteed income? I loved your discussion of anarchism and communism. Shoulder-to-shoulder solidarity is what's needed. There is always the problem, however, that as you concentrate on world issues you

---

* Carol was a co-defendant in Abbie's drug case.

170

lose sight of what demands and changes should be made here within the borders where you say the U.S. doesn't exist.

I understand everything you say about organizing. No one pushes me to do what I do and no one praises me for it or loves me because of it. The only rewards are in the reality of what we are creating. I'm working very hard now getting the advocate center together, but if I'm successful the project will take on a life of its own, independent of me. Nowadays I'm writing funding proposals. The advocate center is an official church project.

The kid says he loves you "all the way up to the top." He is a devout believer in a Santa Claus so we're hanging up stockings the night before Christmas.

Dear one,

In general I'm fit as a fiddle and quite proud of my condition.
I can conceive of "letting everything go" in this condition. I've
been very sentimental lately, missing my old family including
Butterscotch* and junior. Sometimes I walk in the streets alone,
visit a park and watch kids play. There are some kids I relate
to and am having a Christmas party with tree. I cooked a huge
Thanksgiving dinner and am cooking pretty well lately. I'd
like to be a restaurant owner, in addition to everything else.
The past drifts like a cliché out of grasp. I've seen so few people who know who I am. I'm in a sad mood. I feel close to
you and far from you.

The latest reaction to *Book of the Month Club Selection*
made me sad.** Thinking of Jay in New York and the reports
of parties makes me sad. If it wasn't for Angel I'd never get
by Christmas. I understand the meaning of its loneliness now.
Passing birthdays unnoticed. Growing old alone. I feel pretty
well deserted by everyone. Max doesn't want to meet and
neither do you or one or two others. Other things haven't
panned out. These are rough months for me. The marriage,
I should mention, is to overcome some technical problems.
Actually it doesn't alter my feelings about anything. If you
change your mind and decide to come—I hope so, actually, but
am not pressing.

I listen to all the tapes over and over . . . it dulls the mind.

* Butterscotch was our dog.
** This was mentioned in the original of my letter of November 26,
but omitted here.

I guess I'm sad you're not coming. Don't change your mind just 'cause I'm sad about it. The honesty of your reluctance would come out as fast as it has in the past. It's not worth it unless you're totally committed.

I have getting-caught haunts. I awake startled and picture these bulldogs with guns standing over me. I think they'll kill me right off. I say it 'cause it would save them loads of problems and people will believe anything.

Somehow the police and government lying is still an oddity to me. Can you believe that!! I'm such a juvenile. I guess I picture getting caught or a violent death since I have no way of conceptualizing myself at sixty-five or seventy years old. I like to picture myself in comparison with old people I like but everything fails. I would like to see forty through—just two more years, shit, I never thought I'd see that. I have two teenaged children now!! * In seven years my son will be twenty-one. I could be a grandfather any day.

War is inevitable and it's got to pull the U.S. in. If Jackson gains speed for the Democratic nomination he's far in front. He seems too obvious and has the "right" politics to mend party bridges. He doesn't really offend too many. Watch Teddy Kennedy's reaction to him. He's already got Meany. I met Jackson in Miami. He's an incredible Hawk. He'll be Boeing Aircraft's man in the race with rampant support of all West Coast munitions manufacturers. He's got Pentagon support. Jews love his stand on the Mideast, and he's anti-Russia. He's peddling himself as a Truman-type anticommunist. It seems that he and the interglobal politics are perfectly suited for global confrontation in the Mideast. Ford is Eisenhower-dumb, but the sort of dumb that somehow manages to avoid or at least postpone war.

The U.N. is so beautiful. They are exposing the contradictions

* By a previous marriage

of U.S. imperialism contrasted against its lofty rhetoric. Almost every vote now exposes the "Fascist bloc" and the traditional club, U.S., Chile, Israel, Bolivia, Haiti, is emerging in all sorts of votes, not just the Mideast.

I've had two more friends in the IRA arrested. I'm going to mail this now. I'm uneasy about all these letters. Everything's so unstuck in time I'm not sure of any of my emotional world. I'm sending it all, hesitatingly, but wanting to correspond, to see you, to talk. I'm floating in an uncharted sea waiting for the inevitable crunch of the propeller blades at the end of the tunnel.

I've just read your letter of the 12th. You are so unhappy that now I am in the depths. Should I visit you? This letter contradicts everything in your other recent letters.

Don't you think if I could see you without hiding I would in a minute. The trip is just beyond my resources at the moment. You never seem to believe that.

You and america are the only humans with the power to make me unhappy. I'm so sad. Hon, you make me so sad. I cannot really imagine what your life is like, cast adrift like that. You deserve the kid as much as I do. If you are forced into a marriage out of loneliness, maybe you should have him. I want him and I need him but we could work something out. Do you want me? Do you need me? I should not come out of sadness, but if you need some sign from me, if you are desperate for me to come, I will.

I mean, when I read your other letters I thought, "That would have been a fine trip. Going to all that trouble for him to tell me he's in love and married!" You must realize that did not make me regret my decision.

But is the sadness the underlying truth? You make me feel unworthy of your love.

Are you lost? What shall I do? Shall I rescue you? If you think I can, I will.

Hello:

Stoned out of freedom gourd, lying on bed scratching at false identification scattered around. Kristofferson tape (thank-you ma'am) moaning, crooning, in the background. I was talking with some folks here yesterday. I laid out ideas and was so buzzing I almost told them the secret to teach a point, but I didn't. What an incredible high, though, knowing.

I'm too stoned to write coherently. I'm beating around the bush. I'm crying a little. . . . If I ever die, hon, write on the tombstone "He died in the streets." I'd like that. I have no, repeat, no idea why I'm crying but I know it's about us and kiddo. This communicating is very hard. I suppose the reality of forever changing is setting in and I think I'm sad about a lot of things. For instance, feeling cut off from creative people and not having the right people to teach what I know. God, it's something, maybe not a lot.

For instance, I was talking about linear growth as opposed to expansion growth. Like Western thought says Birth, Infancy, Childhood, Adolescence, Young Adulthood, Old Age, Death—and everything gets overclassified. How I hate words like *work* and *retire* and *man* and *woman* and *young* and *old* and *brave* and *coward* and *sick* and *healthy*. All this is triggered by a junk book entitled *How to Retire at 41*. These people were urging me to read it as very sensible, and I went into one of my "extreme raps," and said it wouldn't mix with my consciousness. It should have been called *Fuck Work* or *Death Before Work* or best, *How to Retire at Birth!* I really liked the last.

The conversation got very intellectual and I was so sharp. At times I can't figure it out, what's gained. They already think I'm a cross between Aldous Huxley and Tarzan, so why impress? I figure I'm a teacher and I like to teach and I don't care who or how. I can't believe I'm such an egomaniac. I'm *such* an egomaniac I figure if I am an egomaniac then it's a good quality!! How's that. Anyways, I told them in the New Land people will grow via gestalt expansion instead of linearly. People will go around getting acquainted by asking "Who are you?" rather than "What do you do?"

I'm so disoriented and I'm tripping, I think, but nice. Like I see your face and we're tripping and you say, "Oh, I'm having a good time," and your nose is stuffed and the words come out your nose and it sounds so funny and always made me laugh. The way we used to trip and get so into each other's head and talking was so much fun. . . . Like for hours and so deep and you'd shift consciousness and say, "Oh, I'm having fun," and I'd say "Me, too," and we used to smile at each other. I can never love like that again. I'm pretty sad.

Yes, I haven't written in a while. In fact I was saving letters hoping I could figure out a "stance," a "direction." Goddamn it, I'm still up the tree. I guess you're right not to come. The psychological dilemmas could be increased for both, and then there's our "curiosity" about each other and fear of so much more change. I think maybe it's so hard for us to know each other exactly. I marvel sometimes about human existence, how I've been so close to you for so long and how I don't know you. I read your letters two or three times then I hear stray bits and pieces about you. They *never* jive. You're as much a myth to me as I to you I suppose.

To remind you, love, I'm definitely doing O.K. on this road. It is the greatest challenge I've ever crossed. I'm definitely up to it. Moxie I haven't called on. Even all these feelings toward you and junior—they're making me feel so human. Please don't worry and keep your chin up. You could not bungle visit, except emotionally.

There *are* other people trying to help. You are still the center of the defense but it seemed to be weighing on your shoulders. If others can spell you, why not? I could never be dependent on one person in this condition. Also remember my past letter saying how the past was my biggest burden, naturally, and you're my strongest tie. I expect you to survive in style. If you crack you will diminish in my eyes. I expect you to be strong. We should make a contest out of it—whatever you choose. I want you to live and be happy. If there is pain between us, let me have it. Do you understand I cannot live with your un-happiness. I want it as my crown of nails. I'll be your cuddly little saint, tootsie. I mean it. Stop following the crack-up trend. You're heavy and if I was there I'd kick your bottom!

Hi honey,

I'm listening to Gladys Knight and Jimmy Cliff.

Tomorrow is the decision of the judge. My heart is heavy. It's been a while since I've felt totally helpless about the possibility of your ever being able to be yourself. Who knows what our future will be.

Angel is performing the services of a guardian angel. She must be a terrific security asset. You need someone to watch over your wild soul and spirit.

The kid is in good shape. He had an intestinal virus last week, so I took him to a clinic. What a down trip. It seems almost better to suffer with disease than withstand entire days waiting at the clinic.

Over the Christmas–New Year's period I finished a long-delayed *Ms.* article about prison families, but I'm not happy with it and I don't think they'll publish it.

Goddamn, I'm learning the art of foundation hustling in a few weeks of practical experience. It was a job I feared and took on only because I knew if I didn't do it, it wouldn't get done. So I got myself named **Project Director**, to impress the foundations, and I set about it, learning new techniques each week. At the beginning a lot of people told me it was all personal contacts and who you know. It took me a while to discover that was true. But I'm also in a better position for that than the others. I've raised $3,500 so far, a big milestone for me, from three separate grants. Our goal is $14,000 which is peanuts compared to what other groups ask for, although it seems like a lot to me. The fund-raising is a real challenge, and I love it. I love my work.

179

But there is so much shitwork to do with the kid and the household and the IRS problems that I am always rushed. There is not enough time in the day for the eighty-nine levels I operate on. The organizing is my favorite activity, a rock which enables me to believe in the value of other things, like writing.

Elaine [Markson] has been trying to sell my welfare book outline but the publishers say they are more interested in a personal book by me. It seems to me that with the depression a paperback book on welfare would sell, but I guess nobody considers poor people a good market. The subject of poverty seems to depress everybody who is not poor . . . not a very original discovery. It's treated almost the way sex used to be by magazine and book publishers: unmentionable. You can see loads of open-crotch shots on any newsstand now but search in vain for a description of the life of 30 percent of the population. I'm flattered the publisher's interested in a book by me about me. But . . . feel a certain reluctance, although the moola is tempting. I'll have to mull it over slowly, 'cause writing about me is not what I want to do. I'm like the butterfly who emerges from a cocoon and longs to fly off but is told that before she can fly off she must describe, publicly, her battle out of the cocoon. I do have things to say, but I want to choose my own forms. I can't stand the personal first-person anymore. I've done enough of that.

A twenty-year-old boy flirted with me at a party and—I loved it! Some parties and other experiences are giving me a heady feeling! Last time I felt so popular was my senior year in high school and first year in college. I realize I have a pretty wide circle of acquaintances. At the same time I'm more resigned to loneliness than I used to be. Few people are interesting enough to spend a lot of time with.

Suitcase atomic weapons are on the way, the radio says.

So what else is new?

Jane Alpert got a three-year sentence. Big interview with her in the *Post*. Awful. She puts down the left and stands by her statement that she will mourn no more for the Attica 41.

It's almost a year since we've seen each other. Could I just blow your mind and we both fall in love again—our two new selves? Mayer and I reminisced about you last night, reviewing what he calls your charming seductive qualities. We could both see the twinkle in your eyes very clearly.

The hearings will not be over until the end of February. The judge's latest move was to ask the CIA for wiretap information on you. She referred to the recent disclosures of CIA domestic activities, which have been all over the papers. I think the CIA will deny any surveillance of you and she will render her decision after that. Even though the CIA has admitted to ten thousand files on U.S. citizens, I expect them to deny wiretapping you. That's the way the cookie always crumbles.

Lo luv—

Hectic life, cold day. The humdrum life under that J. Alpert experienced is not my experience at all. A woman friend of mine was reading the J. Alpert story as I walked in. Asked me if I read it. Everyone commenting how strange it must be to be someone else and live underground. . . . Guess so!

Rethinking Erica Jong's book now that I've finished it. It gets pretty bourgeois after awhile. All this introspective crap and she probably deserves the string of losers. There's a part of me, Brandeis, Jewish, Europe, that can identify with her, and at times she's funny and clever with the words—the gift of gab, but she's so involved with her clit. I don't know, I'm waiting for someone to explain the revolutionary significance of feminism. I think you're the only one that could, really. I mean, do feminists take stands on the Mideast, Latin America, or are they just a bunch of pigs fighting over a throne, an irrelevant struggle between men? I think to be consistent they would have to. The best are going to be the inconsistent ones. The adventurers. Hoping to hear your views of *Fear of Flying,* anyway.

The *Post* piece on the hearing makes me pessimistic about changes. I thought it was stronger. Don't worry, I expect nothing. If every day is like yesterday then I'd live contented forever. I felt close to you this morning after waiting all weekend for your letter.

love, caterpillar

I liked *Fear of Flying* because it made me laugh and distracted me one Saturday night when I was stuck at home with kiddo. I would be proud if I could write a book which could do these two things. But I would not have bothered to write about the book if you hadn't kept mentioning it. It really left me cold. I didn't learn anything from it, Maybe if I had read it at another time in my life I would have reacted differently.

My general feeling is that Jong is being praised for what Doris Lessing accomplished long ago, viz. expressing the consciousness of the modern white Western educated woman. When I skimmed through *The Golden Notebook* (it is too long and verbose to read page by page; I prefer skipping around) I felt that a new world had opened to me. I identified completely with the characters and learned from their experiences. The description of sexual experience there I found mind-blowing. I had never before read about sex from the viewpoint of "another woman like me." Lessing does not have such a great sense of humor, in fact maybe none at all, which is probably why you can't read her. I did get some real belly laughs from Jong—the heroine is like a female Portnoy—but I couldn't identify with any of the characters. Jong's heroine's relation to her work and her creativity interested me more than her sexual activities—especially since they were so unsatisfying and also unsalacious. The story that most interested me is the story that begins at the end of Jong's book, which is what Lessing has written about: independent women. When I read Lessing two years ago I was reading about my future. When I read Jong now I am reading about my past.

I've seen Erica Jong on television and she seems like a nice person.

184

I'm always on the lookout for new female writers. The only fiction I ever read is by women. Colette is my favorite writer. I admire her life, her character, and her writing. What a figure to emulate. I haven't yet found a contemporary female author who can compare to her. Her books are surprisingly difficult to obtain here, though. I've been searching for more of her short stories, but have had no luck, perhaps because she's French.

I want to write fiction so much and I fear that I will never get a chance to give it the Big Try, which requires bread. I ain't rich like Zelda, and I sure as hell don't want to end up like Sylvia Plath. Even Colette didn't have to contend with a small child before she was an established writer. I, by the way, could never get into Plath or the story of Zelda. I know that despair trip too well. Big fucking deal. No matter how sensitively intuited, despair doesn't turn me on or teach me anything. Woman as victim is the oldest story going. And I don't like the cult glorification of the suffering artist either.

The best thing I've ever read on the subject of women's liberation is Virginia Woolf's essay, "A Room of One's Own." She says "a woman must have money and a room of her own if she is to write fiction." Imagine what a ridiculous goal "writing fiction" is for a welfare mother! I think that's really what pushed me into organizing. I want to make it possible some day for women like me to become artists.

I've had a lot of lucky breaks lately. Dig this. I got two fortune cookies, in two different Chinese restaurants in the same week, with the same prediction. It was in different print, so not even the same company. Here it is: "An offer of change which will prove most important to your Future." Ah, those Chinese. You would not believe this manic phase, like four hours of sleep a night, twenty projects popping.

About Frances. She should be taught that keeping some secrets and developing your sense of commitment to someone you love whose life is at stake solves more problems than a fistful of dope. It puts you in such a super elite but you have to do your honest share. She has great mobility and that's an asset. She has to learn to follow through. I told her thrills are never enough, money is never enough, sex is never enough. The only thing is to have a big sense of commitment so all that other stuff gets put into a context. There are no thrills for thrills' sake. There are only thrills for experimentation, for putting everything to use for what I call revolution—you don't waste your life, you don't waste a single experience.

High there!

I think of you too, everyday. So much of our early romance comes back to me as I recall your earlier organizing experience. I remember you, dressed always in the same old clothes, running around the city on various errands. I remember you always on the phone and your trancelike preoccupation as I talked to you. Now I am preoccupied when the kid talks to me. Now I dash through streets, keep an appointment book, and am essentially alone all day, darting from one appointment or task to another. Between grocery store and foundation, daycare center and apartment, advocate center and Xerox store, clinic and meeting room. Between public and secret. The sight of a fire in the toilet will be among the kid's early impressions of childhood, to be recalled with dewy eyes.

My life goes in spirals and twists of pleasure and pain. I find that as the spiral grows I become stronger and better able to endure the pain each time it comes 'round. I seem better able to deal with depression. It comes, usually, after I have completed some project and want to relax, to have a good time. When that doesn't happen I begin to feel sorry for myself and sort of go on strike. But no matter how I pursue amusement I usually fail, and bored, go back to work on my next project. On and on like that. There is a certain guilty pleasure to the lay-back periods.

Sometimes when I'm down I glance through the *Autobiography of St. Teresa of Avila*. I was originally curious about her ecstatic trances (as in the Bernini statue) but discovered she was also a good organizer. She founded an order of poverty

when the Church was very corrupt. Three-quarters of her
book is garbage, the product of the period and the culture, but
the rest is fascinating. She says the Devil will urge you to resist
the sin of pride by not acting. He will say to you, "What
makes you such a hotshit that you think you can accomplish
this?"

Someone in London sent me the Agee book on the CIA.
It's the most daring exposé of the CIA yet published. The
author was an agent for twelve years and he names names of
other agents. I wish the Senate hearings on the CIA would start
before your hearings end, but it is unlikely. I don't expect the
CIA to hand over anything at next week's hearings.

Dave Dellinger told me that in the *Dellinger* vs. *Mitchell*
suit, which came out of the Chicago trial, the government has
been forced to hand over volumes of FBI surveillance material on radicals. The suit has received very little publicity so
far because access to the material is limited, by court order,
to the attorneys in the suit. We are seeking to determine what
date the material goes up to because it is certain to contain a
lot of stuff about you.

Junior and I went to Cora Weiss's house for dinner the other
evening. I had called her on behalf of the advocate center. The
guest of honor was a Third Force Vietnamese man, and later,
after he talked, Dave offered a toast to you as "someone who
is missing." I was very moved. The kid had a good time and
made friends with some of the rather distinguished guests.

Junior sends his love. He is gorgeous and can count to ten.

love, your opposite number out there in the CHAOS.

Did you see Ford's budget? At least two more years of massive unemployment ahead. More people now talk about war in the Mideast. The Arabs will be blamed for the depression at home, instead of the oil companies who are tripling their profits. Anyone who objects to the U.S. jumping in to save Israel will not only be accused of anti-Semitism but of preventing a return to prosperity at home, of being against the working class.

You ask me to explain the revolutionary significance of feminism to you. Well, I could just as easily ask you to explain the revolutionary significance of the PLO to me. I'd feel more pro-Arab if I knew the Palestinians were for the liberation of women. There was Leila Khaled once, a few years ago, but what else is new? I would like to believe the more radical factions within the PLO are struggling against the traditional Moslem treatment of women, but I do not know. If they are, you don't hear much about it. The PLO receives a lot of money from Qaddafi, the young, "progressive" ruler of Libya, who supports so many radical Arab causes. He is so pure in his religious fervor that women in his domain are confined to the house and the veil. I read a quote from him saying women who don't wear veils are prostitutes. And you know how much I loved Algeria, another "progressive" socialist country. There were no women in the shops, cafés or streets of Algiers. From Cleaver's apartment you could look down and see the balcony of a nearby building where children played and women hung out the wash behind walls, always behind walls. That's what happened to the brave women who fought for their country's liberation.

It is staggering to think that here we argue about who does the dishes while in a third of the world's countries women can't even argue about leaving the house. As I write this it occurs to me that the psychosexual revolution may be the ultimate one, destined to complete itself only after imperialism is defeated. I hate to say that, but I look around and see men firmly in control of real power, not only economic, but military. In the real world power is intimately linked to violence. I believe the defeat of imperialism around the world will be accomplished through armed struggle, and right now women are not prepared to participate equally in that struggle. Although we are 53 percent of the world's population, we are still a sleeping giant, with relatively few of us aware of our potential to change the world.

I don't think we can wait until all the women can defeat all the men. I think we have to go for little victories wherever we can find them, and I think we can find them in the burgeoning revolutionary movements around the world which claim to be working for human justice. Women have a responsibility to make sure the concern for justice applies to women as well as men. I think these movements will eventually defeat imperialism, but women will not share in the victory unless we have established our leadership during the struggle. That's the most difficult part, establishing and maintaining feminist leadership in what is a male-dominated movement in most parts of the world. It's a challenge we cannot afford to ignore. Whether we work separately or in the ranks of mixed organizations, all of us will progress a lot faster if revolutionary men and women share the same goals and the same targets.

The more I write about this the more muddled it seems to become, n'est-ce pas? If women opt for complete separation we have no identity problems but we may not achieve meaningful change. If we opt for anti-imperialist struggle we risk losing our bid for self-determination. It ain't easy. I'm sitting in some no-man's land between separatist feminists and the women on the left who, for the most part, exhibit little feminism. I bounce back and forth like some activist ping-pong ball.

My friend Leah [Fritz] is a wise feminist and we often argue about all this, but we never seem able to resolve anything. It is easier for me to act it out, step by step, than to analyze all the strategies for change. I, myself, am much more comfortable working with women, just as I feel more comfortable arguing with Leah than presenting you with a feminist analysis. You said once that women are not trained to compete. When women talk to each other they don't compete, they share information. I think that's why women are much better in collective situations than men.

The act of women grouping is the beginning of the revolutionary process. In China when Mao's army liberated a village one of their first acts was to bring women together in "Speak Bitterness" sessions, where women recounted the horrors of their past. These sessions gave women the courage to renounce their former roles and to become activists on behalf of other women. They were the beginning of the women's movement in China. This happened in a nation where foot binding was practiced for a thousand years and outlawed only a generation earlier. Foot binding actually persisted into the forties, when the communists had difficulty eradicating it. They succeeded only after they abandoned a punitive approach and educated people about the practice.

The contrast between the Arab countries and China reminds me that the future is all in our heads, and I choose to be optimistic. I don't usually share these thoughts with you and I sense a certain reluctance because feminism is so, well, personal. To me it's more a state of mind than a set of well-articulated principles. It's the realization that you're not a piece of shit, that you are indeed, first-rate; it's falling in love with yourself and being the hero of your own adventures; it's knowing you're not the moon's pale reflection but the sun, burning. It's being aware that you can change your life, and doing it. It's believing women can change the world. Understand, man?

Hello,

This is going to be my most hectic period in a year. I'm not starting off good either. Four days ago I broke into cold shivers and spasmodic pain. I've had a high fever for four days and my eyes feel like they've been twisted in their sockets and refuse to return to their correct position. I haven't been this bad off since that hep bout.* I get out of bed only to piss. I rarely shit as I hadn't eaten for three days but this morning I woke up from a disgusting dream with you and Butterscotch in it and I keep spitting up pieces of glass. Then I said out loud, "softboiled eggs," which I generally detest, them sort of reminding me of squashed fetuses. But I had two, and feel the fever subsiding some. I did read a lot though. An absolute terror story (I think it triggered the dream) called *The Painted Bird* by Jerzy Kosinski, about a ten-year-old boy lost in Eastern Europe during the Nazi period. A Jewish boy. He's got black curly hair and brown eyes in a region where there are only blond-haired, blue-eyed peasants filled with superstition. It made my blood curl. There's not a happy moment in the book.

I really got into *Tales of Power,* the last Castaneda book. I get a special sense when I hold it that this book (the quartet) is a modern classic. I have no doubt it's authentic. I love Don Juan much more than those shmooroos from India. Them you can wrap all up in one white sheet and hang in a Bo tree.

I am very hung up for bread. If the depression is bad above ground, underground it's just ridiculous. Why hair dye alone has doubled in price!

* In 1969.

Enjoyed *Voice* piece on Patty Hearst. She's doing O.K., all right. I have a theory as to her movements but don't even want to express them in a letter. It's funny, but someone who's been hunted can obviously make a good hunter. It's just like any other life activity, you get to know the ropes.

I find movement people much better for outlaw activities, despite original reservations. Everyone else has to load up on the Valiums and pray. They seem to be off-tune to the risks and fun of it all, you know, that special combination that, along with dedication, urged us into the streets in what you called "that grand adventure."

Two days later. I'm recovering—incredible case of flu. I'm reading in papers about deaths from it. I believe it. I can only be on my feet for about ten minutes before I have to sit down. I dropped eight pounds and have cold sores all over my face. But the fever's gone and I'll be O.K. in a week, I'm sure.

I feel very distant from you. I'm slowly shaking off the past. None of it seems worth the effort to recall. Though it comes to me in flashes at night.

Darling:

I have just been warned that my one free babysitter may not be reliable. That the person might be an informer. I wish there was a way to verify this about the person, but there really is no way. I've got to change a number of things.

Another hearing today. The judge and our lawyers objected to the answer received from the CIA. It was from a CIA lawyer who said, "I have been advised" there is no wiretap material about you and no tapping occurred by the CIA. The judge and our lawyers demanded a categorical "there was no tapping" statement. Gerry [Lefcourt] made a motion to ask for your CIA file but the judge said no, she was only interested in wiretapping. Gerry gave as an example the Bobby Baker case where the notation "june" on certain papers in his FBI file designated material obtained by wiretapping.

The investigator seems to be onto new material but we don't know where it will lead. How I wish you could come back and make all choices out of freedom, and me, too. But I rarely think that way, it's too small a possibility still.

The kid is terrific at playing with blocks. Builds very complex structures which are mostly garages and rockets.

It's a cold, gray month. The entire city is depressed and sick with flu and colds. I'm so depressed I welcome my cold as a diversion. Can't afford babysitters anymore. I get so tired of being alone. Sometimes when I'm in the subway I think, if I faint or get in an accident, there's no one to take the kid. It gets beyond a question of strength. I don't think I'm particularly strong. I just have no choice but to keep pushing on. My work is the only thing that is an up, but the fund-raising is becoming too much. It's removing me too far from the spirit of the thing and I've got to stop soon.

It's February. There are so many people in this city. I'm

just one cell among millions, and who the fuck cares if I waste
my life trapped in this tiny apartment.

                              love,
                              the involuntary solipsist

Hello—

I haven't a thing to write about. Illness ebbing. Thought I had hep again. Tests negative. Just flu, that's going around. Doc says another week to recover strength. I have some fungus growing on my tongue and had some more damage to my liver. Can't imagine needing any of these things later in life anyway. Where the fuck is my bullet? Next year I'll risk more. Will be back at home base tomorrow. Suppose mail from you is there. So will read and respond. Meanwhile, love to junior and you, of course. Hope your winter was mild and coming to an end. The illness has made me depressed. Our correspondence is some sort of anchor to reality. Without it, I sort of flap around.

Dear:

Sorry to hear you were ill. Hope it wasn't the old hep acting up. I am ill now too, with pneumonia. I am very weak and it makes me depressed. I cannot judge how much my mental state is real or the result of sickness. I feel I have nothing to look forward to. I haven't been able to afford sitters and now I learn the free one I had may be a pig! I feel very alone and far removed from pleasure or happiness. Luckily I was able to send junior to my mom. I knew I was ill for about a week, but didn't know what to do with the kid. I was getting cross at him because I couldn't rest with him around. The poverty is making my life a prison, and when I get better I must start working on money plans. I keep looking for fantasies to cheer me up. I like to write, but no time with the organizing. I love movies and parties and going out and laughing, but I feel that will be denied me until I am too old to enjoy it. Sorry to be so self-pitying. I know life can be so good. I know that better than anyone except you. That's why I find it so difficult to tolerate when it's bad and without hope. I wish I could supply us both with money so your risks would diminish.

Lo—

Health coming back strong. I'm feeling tight. Broke a few bricks—tempted to try it with my head—showing off. Conquering all sorts of areas. Got on a horse that had never been rode, got thrown after a minute. Professional did it next. It happened again. Horse was incredible. First we put saddle on and horse went crazy. It ran around for an hour trying to shake it off, rub against trees, then it calmed down and that was that. He accepted it. Next I got on. I wore spurs. They're not as cruel as I used to think. I didn't have any doubts and really wanted to do it. The horse bolted right away and started bucking and yelling. I was determined to stay on. He tried to knock me against the rail though and I guess I got a little nervous and jumped off more than was thrown. I didn't get hurt. It was in a corral with special soft sand. Horses won't step on an animal (humans included). That's nice. I would have gotten back on but I was still somewhat weak from bout with flu. God, what an adolescent!! Angel loved it. I'm really proud of my riding. I've ridden an actual racehorse. You almost never feel the horse yet you're aware of every muscle and his body churning the air, yanking you forward with incredible determination. Of course I miss doing it for junior and taking him. I've been four hours straight on a horse riding in the mountains. It's very thrilling to race over rough, unknown terrain—dangerous too. There's a demoniacal sense to it all. I have a desire—I'm going to study with someone about car engines. We'll see. He says I can learn an awful lot in two weeks.

Enjoyed so much your last few letters. Great description of
Dave Dellinger (our minds are running down same track. I've
been thinking of him recently.) He's a great one. A clutch
player. I also of course like Cora very much. She was solid.
Would be a good candidate for a new party. Excellent presence.

I feel very lefty, not hippie in the least. I like dope, still,
but left alone probably would do it about monthly, not more.
I relate to it as more a social thing. I don't think I'd ever be
antidope but I've noticed when I'm around real "heads," people
who brag about doing dope for ten or twenty years, I think I
have a different attitude. I'm not around many lefties. I feel
a shift inside me though—much more receptive to leftist
rhetoric and analysis. I like reading things like *Passages About
Earth* and *The End of Intelligent Writing* and would find folks
like John Brockman stimulating to talk with, but deep down I
sense Communism—the boring, crass, even building of a party
tied to an international movement—is what people should be
doing. I realize the people that do it will be the worst of us,
in the sense that they'll be the least creative, the tyrants of
groupthink. That's the way the ballgame works. I don't think
people who manage factories are too interesting. Why do we
expect "our" politicians, our party builders, to be more exotic?
Are we trying to make a cowboy movie out of plenary sessions???? Perhaps here is where the underground becomes so
relevant, because at some point in the revolutionary process
they take over the leadership.

I think Mao is right in that the party runs the army, not the
other way around. But I think that's a secondary phase—
obviously the army (underground) has its representatives in all
phases of political organizing. For example I've learned that
the Tupamaros, who are not dead as popular thought has it, are
incredibly powerful and active. They have people in every
level of government, in all walks of life. They have to balance
CIA penetration and power as well as Brazilian might surround-

ing them. Our press aways plays this stuff as so many mosqui-
toes. I think the Third World's really buzzing; we think much
too provincially. The CIA hearings are going to refocus our
energy and attention and remind us that after all what keeps
the whole bowl of Campbell's Soup bubbling is Yankee Imperialism. This is all good education getting us ready for the next
war. I'm actually shocked to find people who do not believe the
U.S. is going to send troops into the Mideast. It's as if they believe the U.S. will never send troops anywhere—rather than
the contrary, which is historically the U.S. has sent troops everywhere. They would have been in Iran in '54 but the CIA pulled
off an assassination and a right coup. They sent Marines pretty
quick into Lebanon in '56 for far less than this. I think they
would have busted the oil embargo in '73 with troops but the
heavy stink of the Vietnam war was in the air and the government was collapsing. Ford, Kissinger and Rockefeller will
probably gain some power as Congress dillydallies with complicated procedural plays and mediocre economic solutions.
They'll be in good shape in a few months to get into gun-boat
diplomacy.

The CIA *is* the foreign policy of the U.S. Rockefeller's committee is naturally a whitewash, what a bunch of jokers. You
know all this. I don't think it can really survive a full-blown
hearing like happened with Watergate. This could be much
heavier. You know, bribing foreign politicians, killing newspaper editors and college professors, running whorehouses
wired for sound, moving napalm and counter insurgency
weapons to military cliques. I think they were into recent
activity in Peru—agitating strike among police. If Peru catches
any agents I think they'll hang'em on the spot. So how can all
this come out—there's real Cloak and Dagger jazz going on.
The CIA is the key to the multinational corporation game
too. They're not a bunch of dummies—people like Helms and
Colby. These aren't your Southern Baptist certified accountants

running around with felt hats and .38 revolvers à la FBI. That's chickenshit peanuts stuff really. It's overseas where all the shit hangs out. It's where you fry the troublemakers' balls, you don't peek in their windows and wiretap their phones.

Have all the news on judge's actions. All this is really great. I'm not in any rush for her to decide. Each little hearing seems to give us more time to prove stuff.

love to all the cook-a-mongoes in the sea,
your friend, Ann Landers

Dear,

It's over a year now. A hard winter. A jittery time.

I am fine and getting back to my old self. The illness I had recently really threw me. It lasted three weeks and the kid was only gone ten days; then I had a relapse of strep throat for another week. Only in the last two days am I really gaining strength. I've gotten pretty close to total loneliness but I've been able to take it in all its bitter variations and I guess I'm surviving O.K. I'm hanging in there. I fantasize meeting you. What a peak experience that will be.

For the moment I've postponed any writing in order to get the advocate center on its feet. Once it's going well I would like to steer it in a more political direction, and write. I think sometimes about getting out of the city, and writing, but these are pipe dreams until I'm satisfied with the progress of the center.

This period has me worried and I'm afraid to ask too many questions. I hope you are well. I'm glad you're not alone. I know you keep saying how much you've changed but you sound to me much the same. Irrepressible. I love you. I wish you could be with the kid. He is a delight. We talk about you a lot. You know what his latest excuse for not going to bed is? (Delivered with wide-eyed bewilderment), "But I don't know *how* to go to sleep."

With all my woes, I know secretly I am lucky. I am so much loved. And although kiddo is the only one around I can actually hug, it's nice to love. It gives a little hope and gorgeous edge to the rim of gray reality. I'm listening to Jimmy Cliff sing

"Sitting here in Limbo . . ." I love that song, also "Many Rivers to Cross," and "You Can Get It If You Really Want . . ." I always dance to that one. I believe it too. Although I'm never sure what it is I really want. Everything, I guess. That pie in the sky. Same things you want: love, adventure, achievement, energy, happiness, and a Cause. That last one, I think that's our little secret.

My soul got warped when I was sick but I think a spark of faith is reviving. For days I sat in bed alone, cut off, reading Xaviera Hollander although I had intended to read Proust (every attempt fails) and listening to the same top-forty songs on the radio, over and over again. During the worst of it I couldn't think of any possible fantasy that aroused my desire. I desired nothing, going on seemed unbearable, and since I couldn't stand to think about any of it, I read Xaviera and Iris Murdoch. Then without any new motivation or dreams I reentered the world. It's a slow build-up. But already there are two or three things I want to do. Maybe by next week it will be the usual twenty.

I'm so lucky to have our boy. He just woke up scared and I took him back to bed. I love it when he puts his arms around my neck and goes back to sleep so trusting. Faith.

Like you, I have faith in our endurance.

Stoically, but with hopes of ecstasy,
oatmeal cookie.

Lo lo—

Well, got your February 16 letter today after a long delay. So sad that you are sick. So sad you're low, feel your life means nothing. I want to help. Please hang on sweetheart. I'm really feeling awful about your state. I've had lots of problems. I know we are in love and will make it. I'm bummed out by your sadness but glad you told me.

This may be my last letter to you for quite some time. I wish I was poetic enough to carve out all my tenderness to you, darlin'. I think everyone knows it. I know Angel does. She's quiet about her emotional life. She's not from a culture that discusses that openly. People are supposed to discover their world through their fingertips. Neat, huh? Different from us. You and me, verbal persons getting off on the sensuousness of the word. There are different types and I think you and I are cut from the same material. I'd like to fantasize that the material is denim. My material selection is very macho. I think I'm macho but with a new twist. Like bragging about a vasectomy. I have a friend. He's a total mach. Carries a gun in his car at all times for who knows why. He once asked Angel to get him a glass of water and I went head to head on him— laying out ideas. I said a man's a sissy if he asks a woman to do anything for him that he could do for himself. That really fucked up his head. There's a whole way of using "challenge" in a constructive way.

I should tell you I'm much more careful and willing to sacrifice pleasure for my security than you might suspect.

I read that Kunstler turned down Patty's mother by saying

"I'll help if you give away everything." Oh, that was so marvelous. He must have felt so good saying that. You must not worry about me. It'll work out O.K. Imagine, I've never told anyone and no one has spotted me. I have been in a room when a friend was reading a magazine, *Newsweek,* and came across my photo. There was no "Hey, this looks like you." None.

I'll make it because "it" is something I've created myself out of left-wing literature, sperm, licorice and a little chicken fat. I love it all . . . .

Time freezes. I'll never change the way I feel toward you. I would love to run my fingers through your hair and my tongue over your nipple. I've done it in my thoughts a thousand times. Your happiness is equal to my own.

Feel my heart, hold my hand. I am with you as time floats by your window like the waves of gentle ocean caresses, licking the walls, creeping in the windows, crawling across the floor to our bed.

The child is our gift, our work. He will be the future, he will lead us into a new century and he will fly on horse's wings like a dashing cowboy and comfort the poor and the lonely. He will be a world-shaker, a champion of all that's right and good. He will be our star. The future is ours.

Love and wet licks,
your party comrade.

Abbie Hoffman was born November 30, 1936, in Worcester, Massachusetts, where he grew up. He graduated from Brandeis University in 1958, and received a Master's Degree in psychology from the University of California at Berkeley in 1960. After abandoning a career in clinical psychology, Abbie became a field secretary for the Student Non-Violent Coordinating Committee (SNCC) in 1963, working on civil-rights projects in Georgia, Mississippi and New England. In 1966, he established Liberty House, a retail chain selling goods of the Poor People's Corporation in Mississippi. A leading activist of the antiwar movement, he was one of the architects of the Pentagon demonstration and the convention protests in Chicago in 1968. Arrested more than forty times, he stood trial in a score of precedent-setting cases, including that of the Chicago Eight. He has written four books, *Revolution for the Hell of It, Woodstock Nation, Steal This Book,* and *Vote!* In March, 1974, facing drug charges in a case in which he claims he was innocent, he became a fugitive. He is presently living, writing and doing political work underground.

Anita Kushner Hoffman was born March 16, 1942, in Baltimore, Maryland. She grew up in Queens, New York, and returned to Baltimore to attend Goucher College, from which she was graduated in 1962. She subsequently studied English literature at Columbia University, and received a Master's Degree in psychology from Yeshiva University in 1966. She has worked as a New York City guide, as a summer security guard at the World's Fair, as a secretary and as a psychotherapist. In 1970, her first novel was published under a pseudonym. She is a founder of the Downtown Welfare Advocate Center in Manhattan.